MILTON J. STEWART

A MAN OF THE SPIRIT

A biography by

John Scott Bennett

John S Bennett

Luke 1:37

PRESS

For

Irma C. Bennett

Our precious mother
went home to her reward June 29, 2008.

Foreword

Milton Stewart burst into my life the first week I arrived in Eugene. It was Sunday morning at Lighthouse Temple, the "mother" church of the Open Bible Standard movement and of Eugene Bible College. Stewart was definitely Pentecostal! While preaching, he was heavily anointed, and at times his style was acrobatic, like evangelist Billy Sunday, who was known for his roving antics. Stewart was hard-hitting on sin, perhaps not traditionally organized or homiletic, but clearly a herald from heaven with a passionate heart for the harvest.

I liked him...a lot! And a good thing it was, for he taught some of my classes at Eugene Bible College, all New Testament epistles of Paul.

I had transferred from a 22,000-student campus in Wichita, Kansas, to enroll at EBC, a school of less than one hundred students. My "dorm" assignment was a small frame home named Hornshuh House with a guy named John Bennett as the dorm "dad." He was single and busy serving Christ as a Christian school principal. Busy was good; that meant less oversight...a luxury we students embraced.

As a teacher, Stewart's textbook was the Bible. Phrase-by-phrase and verse-by-verse he "rightly divided the word of truth." Consumed by a love for God and His Word, and with a passion to prepare leaders for ministry, "Brother Stewart" would often shift gears and preach, rather than teach. But students recognized the anointing of the Spirit in the classroom. They knew—I knew—this was ministry conceived in prayer; we were privileged to hear the message and share the journey of a man walking with God.

Milton Stewart insisted on memorization of Scripture...lots of it. Thank God for that. He valued, modeled, and promoted Scripture memorization and it has helped form my life and ministry. I am forever indebted. Forty years later I still know them, and often sow them into the lives of other people.

Yielding to the Spirit in the classroom seemed as important to Stewart as completing the lecture. If students broke out in a spirit of prayer and intercession, or if prophecy, or tongues and interpretation were manifest, the Holy Spirit was given preeminence. When the Spirit fell upon students, time was given for the move of God. Not all teachers could give leadership, or were as comfortable in such situations, but Milton Stewart recognized students thirsted for 1 Corinthians 12 laboratory experiences.

Outside the classroom, Stewart had already proven himself as a fruitful evangelist and successful pastor. But it was his Ephesians 4:11 office as a prophet that was to most significantly impact my life, a calling not readily recognized by many. He wore the mantle of prophet with courage, humility, and faithful obedience to Christ. History attests to some of the major words he spoke into the lives of individuals and movements; I am confident heaven has recorded many more.

Two examples are personal. In the early spring of 1995, after Open Bible Churches' president, Ray Smith, announced his retirement, Brother Stewart called me to his side. Neither the OBC national convention nor the election of a new president had taken place. Speaking with prophetic authority, he declared and disclosed to me I would be elected the next president of Open Bible Churches. It came to pass. On another occasion, he deposited a significant prophetic word of wisdom in me, one that still directs my ministry and behavior to this day. I am confident this will result in many men, women, and young people being called to vocational ministry.

Milton served as a distinctive leader within Open Bible Churches for over two decades, not the least of which were eighteen years as Pacific Division Superintendent and fourteen years as Assistant General Superintendent. But he will primarily be remembered as a dynamic man of God and mentor of pastors.

M.J. Stewart imprinted his generation for God. He was a spiritual father to many sons and daughters in the faith. I was just one. It is my prayer that this amazing story, this biography of Milton J. Stewart, will result in his mantle and anointing passing to future generations. Amen.

Jeff Farmer
President, Open Bible Churches
Des Moines, Iowa

* * *

Author's Introduction

“The church is asleep, and no one knows how to wake it up!” This clarion call by Milton Stewart rings loudly today. When financial institutions are collapsing, Islamic extremists are threatening, and the morality of our nation and world is rotting us from within, much of the church slumbers on. How can this church, which was born in the intensity of the outpouring of the Holy Spirit nearly two thousands years ago, shake itself and awaken?

Milton Stewart had a clear vision of the church in the last days. It was a scriptural church, filled with and energized by the Holy Spirit. He not only preached that message, he lived it. The hope of a great awakening within the church was a driving force in his life. He was a man with a vision and a dream for bringing God's will “on earth, as it is in heaven.” This book has been written to share the life of this man of God and to pass that dream on to you.

Several years ago, I heard Milton Stewart had been invited to Edmonds, Washington, to speak. It had been years since we had seen each other, so my wife and I made plans to ferry across Puget Sound that Sunday morning. As I thought about our meeting, I wanted to bring him something that would bless his heart.

The previous year for Father's Day, I had delivered a testimonial in our church, giving honor to Milton, my "second father." I took that text, expanded it, and brought it with me when we met that morning at the Open Bible Church with pastors Bill and Karen Clemons. Milton was delighted. I sent a copy to Jan Hornshuh Kent who was alumni director and in charge of Open Bible Churches' Archives at Eugene Bible College. She enthusiastically responded by demanding more "Stewart stories."

As word got around I was writing some things about Milton and Ruth, I kept hearing the refrain, "The Stewarts' lives are a story that needs to be told." The Lord convinced me I was the person to tell that story, so I began. A year later, their daughter Pam Stewart-Adams brought Milton and Ruth to Medford, Oregon for a meeting with our family at Bob and Lynn Stafford's home. My sister Lynn rolled out the red carpet for us all. Our mother, 98-year-old Irma Bennett, sister Eve and I were finally reunited with our friends and beloved pastors, Milton and Ruth. What sweet fellowship! That weekend marked their 65th wedding anniversary, so we were doubly honored to be with them.

When writing a book about someone you love, I am keenly aware that objectivity is a challenge. The impact his life made upon mine, especially through my adolescent years, was enormous. But that is also the testimony of hundreds and probably thousands of people. He is a man who lived wholeheartedly and gave himself fully to the ministry of the Gospel. No one, especially they, will deny the Stewarts have faults, but the purpose of this book is to, as accurately as possible, tell their story to the glory of God, without undue embarrassment to anyone. Milton and Ruth were loyal, not only to Christ and the Gospel, but also to their chosen denomination, Open Bible Churches.

Through the years, the name of the organization has changed from Bible Standard Churches to Open Bible Standard Churches to its current name, Open Bible Churches (OBC). We have chosen to use the modern name throughout the book, except when directly quoting another person or source. The same is true with Eugene Bible College, which began as Bible Standard Theological School and went through several name changes until becoming EBC. Within the denomination, the Stewarts are mostly referred to as Brother and Sister Stewart, or M.J. and Ruth Stewart. To be consistent and avoid parochialism, we are simply, but respectfully, calling them Milton and Ruth. Unless otherwise noted, Bible quotations are from the New International Version, Zondervan Publishing House, 1973.

Most of the stories contained in these pages have been gathered from conversations with the Stewarts. This is their story. If there are omissions, or points of emphasis we have missed, I take full responsibility. The book would not have been written without the help and encouragement of my wife, Karen. She has endured many boring weekends while I sat working at the computer. Having been an outstanding English teacher, her insights and comments have been invaluable. Joan Lumbard read a number of the chapters aloud to catch the flow of the story, then passed on helpful suggestions to me. Jan Kent's interest was the initial impetus in writing a full biography. She has gone out of her way providing help, especially at our 2008 EBC Reconnect. My daughter Julie and her husband Scott Snyder prepared the advertisement for the book to our OBC friends at Reconnect. Julie, also an English teacher, made thoughtful suggestions for the betterment of the text. Pam Stewart-Adams has read many of these chapters to her parents. Her weekly connection with her folks has kept the factual matters of the book on target.

It may be impossible to list all those who have contributed to the content of this book, however, I would be remiss in not acknowledging the help of the following: the Stewarts' other three children, Pat, Bobbi Jo, and John; Don and Ruth Bryan; Ken Brown; Marilyn Brown; Skip and Dawn Ringseth; Charles W. Jones; Clayton and Suzanne Crymes; A. Don Crawley; Eve Skinner; Bob and Lynn Stafford; Surena (Harding) Hines; Jeff Farmer; Bob Laflin; Larry Burke; Lonnie Burke; and those who contributed to the Tributes at the end of this book.

My long time friend, Gwenell (Foster) Zimmerman, has been my faithful editor. Every writer needs an editor willing to confront him. Gwenell has no problem with that, and I thank her for her sacrificial help. She has taken this biography of the Stewarts under her wing and given untold hours correcting and rewriting portions of each chapter. Gwenell continually keeps me focused on the quality of my writing. We both trust the written expression of the Stewarts' story in no way impedes the impact of their lives on all of us.

This biography is, in reality, the story of the grace of God through two very human beings. The months spent gathering information and crafting this book have been rewarding to me, its author. I pray your life will be as enriched in reading this story as mine has been in telling it.

John S. Bennett

* * *

Contents

Prologue

Gold Bar, Washington
Sometime in the late 1940s

The fourteen-year-old girl eagerly jumped out of the car and ran to the registration office. She was told she had been assigned to cabin "D" on the edge of the woods. Grabbing her bags, she rushed over to the cabin to meet some friends from past years and add new ones to the list. Gold Bar camp was the year's high point for Washington Open Bible Churches' youth.

What fun to be away from home in such an attractive campground! She and her girl friends chattered merrily as they chose bunks and stowed luggage. Later that first evening, the scramble of kids that flooded the grounds earlier had dissipated. Cabin lights winked on.

Suddenly, sharp bursts of fireworks exploded outside the cabin door. What was happening? After the initial fright, camper Mardell Varney went out with friends to investigate. Nothing appeared to be damaged, and the only evidence was spent firecracker paper and a bit of lingering acrid smoke. Well, the girls surmised, the boys have arrived. They quieted down eventually and drifted off to sleep.

The next morning, campers gathered for breakfast in the main hall. The camp director welcomed the teens, then announced that a special guest had come to address them. A young forest service ranger stood up in his khakis, boots, hat, navigator sunglasses and badge. "Wow!" Mardell thought, "What a handsome young man to be our own ranger!"

"It's unfortunate," the ranger said, after welcoming the campers, "that we have already had a violation of our forest service rules. As visitors here, you should be reminded this summer has been exceptionally dry. Fire danger is great." As he spoke, the ranger was slowly walking among the tables of young people. "It is my understanding that somebody in this camp set off fireworks last night." He was almost standing beside the teen girl's table now. Looking directly at her, he paused, pointed a finger and said, "I understand that you, young lady, know something about this."

She was mortified! The whispering among the campers was like a beehive, but the ranger continued, "We are working with your camp leaders to bring this matter to a quick conclusion. An announcement will be made as soon as all the facts are brought forward. Please be aware of the fire danger, and let's have no further incidents with matches or fireworks." With that, the ranger turned and walked back to his seat with the camp director.

Feeling the hot flush of embarrassment made that young lady want to disappear. There was no way out, however; the main speaker for the week was already being introduced. "This man is a talented trumpet player, a young preacher from Martinez, California, a man who loves kids. Please welcome to our Gold Bar Camp...Milton Stewart."

Gasp! It was the ranger! With his hat and glasses off, he waved at the teens while they howled their approval. Mardell was flabbergasted, but relieved. Spontaneously, she was out of her seat and rushing to the front. She gave Milton, her evangelist/ranger, a big hug. Even though she had been the object of this set up, she couldn't help but admire and respect the man who made it happen.

One particular camper never forgot that day. A lasting friendship began in spite of the double personality of a speaker and the vulnerability of a camper. The couples of Dan and Mardell LeLaCheur and Milton and Ruth Stewart have enjoyed a friendship through 60 years of the Stewarts' ministry.

Milton loved to preach to and challenge teens to live for God. Each summer, for twenty-five years, he ministered at Open Bible Churches' camps from coast to coast. No doubt many other teens were the objects of his humor. It would be interesting to see how many could relate! Maybe you, dear reader, are one of them.

This biography is written to introduce you to this "Man of the Spirit." May you be blessed and inspired in your own spiritual walk by knowing him better.

* * *

Chapter One

Childhood Imprints

*"Being confident of this, that he who began
a good work in you will carry it on to
completion until the day of Christ Jesus."*
Philippians 1:6

Milton Jennings Stewart's birth on September
27, 1920, seemed as insignificant as the
Oregon town of Dixonville, west of Roseburg, where
his parents lived. Lawrence and Myra Norris Stewart
were trying to make a living in the harsh years
following World War I, before the '20s started to roar.
Lawrence was an intelligent and energetic young
man who, like so many others in Dixonville, worked
in the woods. He was very positive and possessed a
good sense of humor. Myra was a five-foot-two ball
of fire who loved her newborn son dearly. She was
determined to raise him with the worthwhile values
her parents had passed on to her.

Myra's folks lived not far away on a two-acre plot in Dillard south of Winston and Roseburg. Milton and Martha Norris, better known as Milt and Matt, had homesteaded 160 acres in the foothills of the coastal range, but preferred living on their small plot closer to town.

They raised an assortment of animals including ducks, geese, sheep, cattle and goats. They also grew some of the best melons in the valley. As grandparents, they figured prominently in being a stabilizing influence in their grandson's early life. Their house was a second home for Milton, whether for a weekend, or the better part of a summer.

Two years after Milton was born, his father left home, never to return. The couple divorced and, over the years, Lawrence went through a series of four or more marriages. Because he usually did not live far from Milton, his son would visit or live with his father and one of the stepmothers for a period of time.

When Milton was about four years old, he lived in his dad's home with a stepmother who simply despised him. One day, without warning, and in a fit of rage, she grabbed Milton, lifted him up to the sink and turned on the water. She held his face under the faucet, attempting to drown the boy. He was strong for his age and fought back mightily. When she let the frantic child go, he lost no time getting out of reach of this abusing adult. The battle had gone on long enough to more than traumatize Milton, and he considers the memory of that event to have permanently seared his psyche.

A few weeks later, the stepmother's parents invited the relatives for a Thanksgiving dinner. Although Milton wasn't feeling too well, he had no choice but to be a part of this large gathering around the table for the festive meal. As the dinner continued, his stomach felt more and more queasy. Finally, he couldn't hold back any longer. Erupting uncontrollably, he showered the table in front of him with vomit. What a mess! The disruption and chaos that ensued was about the worst thing anyone could imagine. So much for the great family get-together. In his four-year-old mind, and for years later, he thought of that event as pay back for the near-drowning abuse of his father's disturbed wife.

Those early formative years were fraught with difficulties. Physically, he had inherited visible eye problems from his mother. One eye was lazy and drifted toward his nose, giving him a cross-eyed look, and he had a form of astigmatism. These congenital difficulties gave cause for neighborhood children and cousins to inflict bitter teasing. Without a father, and being shifted around from home to home, he endured taunts and loneliness. His mother found waitress jobs to earn what she could to support Milton and herself. Through Myra's single years, Milton spent more and more time in the relatively peaceful atmosphere of his grandparents' house. It became his primary home from age three through the first grade.

His grandmother Matt was a lifelong Baptist who loved the Lord, but due to some quirk in her convictions, would only attend a Baptist church. Since there was none in town, she often hosted Bible studies and prayer groups in her home, but she wouldn't darken the door of the nearby Dillard Methodist Church. When Milton lived with them, she would often get him dressed up and send him to one of the three country Methodist congregations serviced by a single pastor.

From an early age, Milton displayed an unusual curiosity, wanting to know everything about everything. This about drove his grandmother to distraction, but she took a practical approach, teaching him to read before he ever started school. The Norrises had a number of books in their home, which Milton quickly devoured. Grimm's Fairy Tales, Mother Goose, Arabian Nights, and many others were rapidly consumed. His journeys through their little home library blossomed into a life-long passion.

Grandfather's influence on Milton was quiet, but lasting. Early one winter morning, Grandpa Milt bundled his grandson up to help him with the morning chores. Grandpa had the lantern, Milton the bucket, as the two walked through the cold morning mist toward the barn. "Milton," Grandpa said as he turned in the stillness of the morning to face his grandson, "a man is no better than his word. If his word is no good, he's no good." As a quiet man of five feet four inches he was not physically imposing, but his character was legendary.

Grandpa Milt had signed a lease for the use of some land with an owner who did not know him well. This gentleman was in the hardware store talking with the proprietor, when he brought up the subject of Milt's lease. He said he was a bit worried Milt might not fulfill his part of the signed agreement. The hardware man replied, "Well sir, Milton Norris's word is better than any paper you could find." Such was the reputation of Grandpa Milt.

During Milton's first-grade year at Dillard Elementary, his mother, Myra, married a railroad man named Earl McDowell. In the second grade, Milton moved back with his mom and stepfather, continuing to attend the small country elementary school.

Formal school was tough in many ways for the young lad. The desks were all connected together in rows, front to back. From a regular seat in the class-room, Milton seldom could read what was on the blackboard. Sometimes it took a teacher quite a while to discover Milton wasn't able to focus from where he was seated. At this finding, he suffered the further embarrassment of having a special desk provided for him in the front, next to the teacher, but away from his classmates. His eye problems also made him a teasing target for some of the older school kids, especially on the playground.

In the third grade, circumstances changed again for the young boy. He was sent to Coquille, Oregon, to live with his father and stepmother, Edna. Lawrence was a high climber, topping trees for Coos Bay Lumber Company in Coquille. Edna really clicked with Milton, and on top of that, she had a head of glorious red hair. Of the several wives his father had, she was the one who treated him best. He always felt the warmth of her welcome in their home.

In his adult years, Milton's family said his propensity for redheads began with stepmother Edna, carried through to his wife Ruth, and then to his first-born daughter Pam...all redheads.

About the time Milton turned nine, one of the defining events in American history befell the nation...the stock market crash of 1929! He returned to Dillard to live with his mother and stepfather who found himself desperate for work. Because Earl was an employee of the Southern Pacific Railroad, he had to move his family wherever the railroad had an opening. This began a seemingly impossible journey from job to job and town to town through Milton's fourth-grade year in school. In one year, he found himself in Dillard, up the Oregon coast to Tillamook, down to Marshfield, over in the Willamette Valley to Albany, back to Dillard, and finally ending ten miles north, in Roseburg. Seven school changes in at least five towns within one school year. It sure felt good to get back close to Grandpa Milt and Grandma Matt.

Milton's mother Myra was quite short, but she was a knockout! Folks in the area used to say the popular song of the time was written with her in mind.

> *"Five foot two, eyes of blue,*
> *Oh what those five feet could do!*
> *Has anybody seen my gal?"*

With her blonde hair, blue eyes and beautiful five-foot-two features, she turned heads wherever she went. But her physical beauty wasn't her defining characteristic. Myra had a mind of her own and a will to back it up. You didn't push her around, and what she thought was right, you might as well believe, was right! Milton remembers when his mom and step dad got into an argument while gardening in the back yard. It took several weeks for the wounds to heal in Earl's head where Myra had planted the rake tines. She wasn't usually mean, but Milton and everybody around knew who was running the ship. In raising Milton, she taught him how to be respectful, honest, well-dressed, clean and neat. She cared a great deal for her only child, but had a hard time giving him personal praise or displaying affection.

The summer between his fourth and fifth grades, his parents found housing a block and a half away from Grandpa Milt and Grandma Matt's home in Dillard: a railroad section house painted the mustard-yellow signature color of the Southern Pacific Railroad. Though not large, it was comfortable and downtown.

Milton's fifth-grade year in Mr. Rohner's class at Dillard Elementary was one of his best. Seeing the potential and intellectual drive Milton possessed, Mr. Rohner gave him opportunities to develop his skills. Since Milton was an exceptional reader, it was arranged for him to go to the third-grade class-room where he tutored younger students, under their teacher's direction. Not getting the attention of his stepfather at home, Milton thrived under the tutelage of this male role model who understood and cared for him. However, his personal reading exploits hit a significant bump in the road when, near the end of the school year, he realized he had read every book in his elementary's library. His grandparents had some adult books he hadn't cracked yet, so he turned to Homer's *Iliad* and *Odyssey* and Arthur Conan Doyle's mystery books. Instead of completely stopping his reading at school, he began devouring old textbooks...math, science, whatever...simply anything he could scrounge up to read.

In the fall of his sixth-grade year, his parents took him hunting, along with seemingly half the town. It wasn't for sport; it was the annual pilgrimage for meat to sustain families in the coming winter. Neighbors and relatives loaded their vehicles, drove to a favorite hunting ground, set up camp, and spent a week or more in the game-laden countryside of west-central Oregon. Milton, his uncle and stepfather were part of this fall spectacle. Tragic news awaited them when they returned home with their game. Their section house had burned to the ground. With no fire trucks in the area, nothing of their personal possessions had been saved.

Grandma and Grandpa Norris still had their house on the homestead land in the costal range of the Cascades. They opted to move there in order to leave the Dillard house for Myra, Earl and Milton. At the beginning of the Great Depression, it was a most trying time for a family with meager resources, but the small house served as their refuge through Milton's eighth-grade year.

As the seventh grade began, every day was a new adventure. Junior and senior high students in Dillard hopped on a bus and commuted all the way to Roseburg. What a thrill it was to have a new library he could explore! But what most caught his eye was the junior high music room. It was full of instruments the students could try. Since some of his classmates had begun playing already, Milton thought it would be right up his alley to join them.

He went poking around town to see what he could find. Within a half block of his home was a second-hand store he knew, but had never looked for an instrument there. As he searched through the familiar store, he spotted an old nickel-plated cornet sitting on a dusty shelf. Examining it carefully, he saw it was complete—mouthpiece and all. He asked the owner if he could try it out. A few blows later, and finding all the valves worked, his mind was made up.

"How much you want for this instrument?" he queried.

"Well, son, for you, just $5.00."

Milton set the instrument down, and slowly walked out of the store. He didn't have $5.00 and didn't know how he could earn it but, one way or another, he was determined to have that cornet. He beat a path home to talk with his Grandma Matt, who was visiting for the weekend, and excitedly told her of his find. Explaining in redundant detail the value, availability, and need of the cornet, he presented his case to his grandma, vowing to pay her back, faithfully practice, and probably never ask for another thing as long as he lived. It must have struck a chord with Grandma, as it didn't take her long to find the necessary $5.00, and Milton was the owner of his first cornet.

Seeing his enthusiasm for, and early progress on the horn, his mother and band teacher discussed a local instrumentalist who could give Milton some lessons. This teacher knew a man by the name of Skip Gilmore, an incredible trombone player. Certainly he could help a beginner learn how to play a cornet. So Milton began lessons with a man who had been the lead trombonist for the John Philip Sousa Band. His mom bargained to furnish eggs, bacon, milk and other farm produce in exchange for the lessons. With plenty of practice, Milton's skills grew by leaps and bounds.

Arranging with her restaurant boss for time off, she drove Milton the ten miles to Roseburg for his lessons. Myra and Earl owned a brown Ford Model T roadster with a soft top, which they named "Chocolate Drop." With Myra's lead foot and poor eyesight, it was always an adventure driving to Mr. Gilmore's home. After the lesson, Milton was on his own getting back to Dillard. During the Depression years, there were lots of people needing rides, and folks were pretty generous about picking up neighbors or strangers along the highway. A few times, though, Milton walked the entire ten miles back home.

His mean-spirited uncle made matters even worse. Seeing him walking along the road, he would slow down beside him and holler out the window, "Hey, Milton, are you tired of walking? Maybe you'd better start running then. Ha, ha, ha, ha!" With that, he would speed off, never once giving his nephew a ride.

At age twelve, Milton was in line for an unexpected encounter that would change him forever. When the English evangelist Brymer came to Dillard to hold revival meetings at the neighborhood Methodist church, it became a significant event in the community. Milton, his mom and stepfather were among those in attendance. This evangelist preached the Gospel of repentance and personal faith in Jesus Christ.

The presentation was clear, and the Holy Spirit began working in Milton's heart. On the second evening, he responded to the altar call and gave his heart to Jesus Christ. He was forgiven of his sins, a new joy was alive in his soul, and there was no doubt in Milton's mind that God had changed him. Every night through the week, he was one of several students who were enthusiastically attending and growing in their newfound faith. His mother and stepfather also stepped forward and made a public profession of faith in Christ.

The following week, Brymer was scheduled to be the evangelist at another Methodist church several miles from Dillard. Milton and his friends crowded into the back of a pickup for the short journey to this town's one-room schoolhouse where the meetings were being hosted. Arriving ahead of the start of the service, they talked and warmed themselves around the pot-bellied stove. There was no forewarning for what came next, but as clearly as an audible voice, Milton heard God say, "I want you to preach the Gospel of Jesus Christ!"

It was so distinct and real, he looked around to see how his friends had reacted to the message. He was surprised to find he was apparently the only one hearing the voice. After a short time, God spoke to his heart again, just as clearly, and with the same message: "I want you to preach the Gospel of Jesus Christ!"

* * *

Chapter Two

Teen Survival

*"The one who calls you is faithful,
and he will do it."*
1 Thessalonians 5:24

The salvation and call to ministry of twelve-
year-old Milton became buried deep within this
misunderstood young man. It would be years before
he told anyone of God speaking so distinctly to
him. His perception of others' attitudes toward him,
as he entered his teen years, was not encouraging.
Relatives and friends had severely teased him, calling
him cross-eyed, and other demeaning names, which
conveyed their opinions that he wouldn't amount to
anything. From now on, he would avoid being hurt by
simply keeping quiet about his salvation and God's
voice calling him to "preach the Gospel."

At a time when he most needed the spiritual direction of the church and people of God, he received

little. There was no follow up and little encouragement to pray or grow in the knowledge of God and his Word. Mercy Buell, though, was one bright spot in the life of the Dillard Methodist Church. She taught Milton's Sunday school class with a warm and caring nature. She and her husband, Fred, owned a local grocery store and were strong witnesses for the Lord in the community. Other than the enthusiasm of her spirited love for the Lord, Milton did not experience another adult who nourished his spiritual life at Dillard Methodist. When Sunday arrived at the McDowell home, it was basically Sunday-go-to-meetin' time, for more social reasons than Christian. Without spiritual roots, the family's fresh experience in Christ began to diminish.

Myra strongly influenced her son, even though she was silent about spiritual values. Personal integrity was paramount; the practice of honesty, even when it hurt, was a cardinal rule in the household. She always dressed well and expected her son to do the same. They may not have had enough money for the latest styles, but what was worn was clean and neat. Hard work was a virtue. From the time he began taking lessons on the cornet, he learned to be diligent in practice. If he wasn't, those wonderful lessons with Mr. Gilmore could stop. The same discipline carried over into his classes, and homework was done with focus, quality and timeliness.

Voracious reading continued throughout his school life. With his eye problems, he was not comfortable reading for long stretches of time, but his hunger for knowledge kept him going. Later in life, he could devour a Reader's Digest magazine from cover to cover, then give the title of each article, forward or backward. Histories and biographies remained tops on his checkout list at the library.

During the summer of 1934, in the heart of the Depression, his stepfather was transferred to Powers, Oregon, where the family lived for that school year. Milton became a regular attendee at the services of First Christian Church, but his parents rarely worshiped with him. For recreation and financial gain, he and his Irish band buddy, Pat Hennesey, would set up a donation can on the sidewalk of Main Street and blow their horns for the locals. That earned them some attention (much of which was good), and a bit of spending money for ice cream. When they hungered for pure fun, there was always the nearby Coquille River for a great cold swim.

His cousin, Jack, and his mother lived in Powers where the two boys became great buddies. They insisted on doing everything together, so when Jack heard Milton had measles, he felt left out. Going over to the McDowells' home, Jack spent enough time with Milton to catch the malady. The two friends shared the weird pleasure of suffering through the stages of the disease together...much to the dismay of their parents.

The next year produced another move, a significant change...to the big city of Eugene. Myra scoured the papers and realty offices for a place to live. It was

1935. Not only was money scarce, housing was in a great state of flux. Myra came upon a listing that seemed unbelievable. A two-bedroom house in the River Road area was for sale for $5.00 down and $5.00 per month! It took only a quick visit to find the house was not a beater, but fairly sound. They put $5.00 down and moved in for what would be their permanent home. Milton put down roots at the Methodist church in downtown Eugene, although Myra and Earl attended only on occasion.

Milton earned A's and B's at Eugene High School, located at 17th and Charnelton, and in his senior year, he checked out the track program. The coach had invited newcomers to compete against the veterans. Aha! This was a sport in which he could compete without being handicapped by poor eyesight. Milton borrowed a pair of shoes and ran the mile against last-year's champion. Incredibly, he won the race, but it nearly killed him. Catching the flu the next week put him out of any practice routine. He never became a part of the team, but always savored that one great memory of winning on the track and enjoyed the thought of what might have been.

Band, again, was his favorite class. In his junior year, he organized an extra-curricular five-instrument German "oom-pah" band to play for school and community events. He bought music for the musicians, and dug up some look-alike skimmer hats. White shirts, black bow ties, and black and white checkered vests, made by some of the mothers, finished off the outfits. Students loved the sound and looks of this popular group, which often was asked to perform at their assemblies. The local Elks, Odd Fellows and VFW clubs came asking for their services and were happily entertained by Milton and his musician friends.

In band class, the two boys occupying the first and second seats in the trumpet section were very talented musically, but undisciplined goof-offs. At the end of their junior year, band director, Doug Orm, had had enough. He announced to his band that he was no longer willing to tolerate the attitudes of these young men. Beginning with the new school year, they would not be part of the band. Milton Stewart would be promoted to first trumpet. Milton loved his band class and considered his director a great role model.

Mr. Orm recommended a highly qualified, but demanding, trumpet teacher for Milton. He learned advanced techniques, including double and triple tonguing. As importantly, he was taught proper stage presence and posture. When Milton graduated from high school, indicating an interest in the University of Oregon, Mr. Orm wrote his letter of recommendation to director Mr. Stein. It stressed that Milton deserved consideration for first-chair trumpet in the U of O band. When Milton showed up in the fall for his first band class, Mr. Stein was there to greet him. After considering the recommendation of Mr. Orm, and giving Milton a brief tryout, he placed this young freshman as his first-chair trumpet man.

Milton treasured his associations with Mr. Orm and Mr. Stein, both strong leaders and accomplished in their chosen field. The respect these two men garnered in Milton's eyes filled an obvious void for masculine mentoring. His stepfather, Earl McDowell, functioned with benign neglect and never developed an emotional father-son connection with Milton. The only memory Milton had of meaningful conversation with Earl was when fixing pancakes together after Myra left early for work.

Life at the University of Oregon was full as he carried an average load of classes, in addition to his band work. A landscaping job gave him some tuition money, but not much for spending. Of course there were interesting girls. Although he wasn't walking in companionship with Christ, his convictions were surprisingly strong. When his literature teacher was comparing types of exceptional writing, she summarized her feelings by telling the class there was no difference between the inspiration of Shakespeare's writings and the inspiration of the Bible. Something within Milton rose up, and he felt like shouting, "No, that's not right! The Bible's different. It's the inspired Word of God!"

One afternoon he was talking casually with a girl he had met in class. They were sitting on the sofa sharing a bit, when Milton mentioned to her, "You know I once used to think I was going to be a preacher." He was not prepared for her reaction. Jumping to her feet, she began to shout and swear at him, ordering him out of the house. She followed him to the porch, continuing the vicious diatribe. As he walked away, he could make no sense of how his words could have precipitated such an outburst.

During the winter of his first year at the U of O, Milton made a discovery that opened an entirely new door for him. One of the downtown churches had an orchestra that played every Sunday night. Since his church did not have regular Sunday evening services, he decided to take his horn and go. The orchestra director Mr. Crook was more than competent in directing and arranging music. Milton liked him and became a regular part of the trumpet section in the Lighthouse Temple orchestra. Across the room in the violin section, was a young lady who took special note of the new college man playing trumpet.

Ruth Phair was a tall young lady in her sophomore year of high school. Her red hair sparkled as she drew her bow and expertly handled all arrangements before her. She was the middle of five daughters born to Bill and Ethel Phair. Her father, raised in Ireland, learned the plaster trade after coming to America. Her mother was a housewife with an amazing array of skills. Not only was she an excellent pianist, but also a trained stenographer. When she married Bill, they first lived a rural life where her professional abilities couldn't be used. They later moved to Springfield, Oregon, where the young family attended a nondenominational mission church.

In Springfield, a serious physical crisis arose when Bill got the hiccups. They weren't the ordinary kind, but carried on for several days. A concerned neighbor told him their pastor prayed for the sick, and Fred Hornshuh Sr., pastor of Lighthouse Temple, was contacted. Arriving at the Phairs' home, he prayed for Bill. God cured the hiccups and, as a result, the whole Phair family began attending Lighthouse Temple. The family was soundly converted, growing in the Lord and finding ways to serve Him.

When E.J. Fulton came to pastor the church, Mrs. Phair thought so much of his messages she took them down in shorthand, typed them up and gave them back to him in written form. The Phairs and their five beautiful, eligible daughters were known as hospitable people, often having the pastors and special guests of the church in their home.

Ruth's mom introduced musical instruments to the girls at an early age. Jane, the eldest, was given violin lessons. The more Ruth heard that instrument, the more she was fascinated by it. Even though she was merely seven years of age, when the violin was left out and unattended, she often picked it up and began trying to play. There was an immediate connection, and her mother made arrangements for Ruth to have her own violin and begin lessons.

Mr. Beuford Roach was an excellent violinist and teacher. After getting all Ruth's self-taught habits out of the way, and insisting upon solid fundamentals, he ably coached Ruth and watched one of his star pupils develop into a skilled violinist. When she reached her junior-high years, her talent was noticed at school, where she began playing for assemblies. The same was true at Lighthouse Temple, and Mr. Crook asked her to become one of the youngest members of his church orchestra. At this time, arrangements were made for Ruth to spend a summer in Portland with her aunt, who had vital connections with the local musical world. Mr. Isaac Lord, one of the finest violin teachers in the Northwest, who had extremely tough requirements, tutored her. Every day she practiced at least four hours, and through the summer, met with her instructor for lessons twice a week. Her love for the instrument and confidence grew by leaps and bounds.

Because Ruth was attractive, poised, talented, and popular at Springfield High School, she was nominated by her sophomore class to contend for queen in the annual competition. When the votes were tallied, she was some short of winning the event, but felt very honored to stand next to the queen as first runner-up. The winter of her sophomore year was when Ruth first noticed Milton over in the trumpet section of her church orchestra. He was a good dresser, enthusiastic, and handsome. She noticed he occasionally stayed for the evening preaching service.

As much as Milton loved playing in the orchestra, he soon felt uncomfortable because of the convicting presence of the Holy Spirit in his life. Inside him there seemed to be no spiritual life. Hearing the Gospel preached, and seeing the joy of the Lord in the lives of these new friends at Lighthouse Temple, served to make the contrast he felt more evident. When invited to play his cornet for the youth group, he selected one of the most familiar hymns he knew, "The Old Rugged Cross." As he got into the piece, sweat began pouring from his face. His heart was pumping from conviction, and he could hardly keep the mouthpiece on his slick lips. When he finally finished and sat down, he not only knew he wasn't right with God, but felt everyone around him probably knew, as well. The struggle was on.

In spite of his discomfort, Milton wasn't about to walk away from Lighthouse Temple, his musical friends, and that pretty violinist with sparkling red hair. One evening after the orchestra members finished playing, they put away their instruments, walked down the back steps through the basement and up the steps to the front of the church. Ruth and her friends found a place to sit. As soon as she was seated, Milton leaned in from the aisle asking, "Would you mind if I sat with you?" She scooted over enough for him, and with that introduction in the spring of 1940, their courtship began.

Milton was now in his first year at the University of Oregon, studying for classes and working part time. On weekends, his cousin Jack would sometimes come from Powers to visit, and the two cousins would double date the Phair sisters, Ruth and Marian. The more time Ruth and Milton spent together, the more they enjoyed one another. One close observer of this budding romance was Milton's mother Myra. She could see the godly character and wholesomeness in Ruth, so she made it a point to give her son a warning: "You can't fool around with that girl, Milton. She's a serious young lady, and she's a Christian."

As Ruth and Milton continued dating, it now seemed right that he would offer a going-steady ring. She gladly accepted and proudly wore it everywhere. After all, it was quite a feat for a high school girl to be going steady with a young college man. Even though Ruth knew her boyfriend was not living a vital life with the Lord, she had a deep sense this was the man God had for her. From her childhood, she believed God had chosen her for a special ministry in his kingdom; she had a biblical name, and a call from her Lord. Just how God would work this out, she didn't know, but she sure was falling in love with Milton. He was lots of fun to be with, and there was a certain honesty about him that was refreshing. If he promised her something, he would fulfill it, regardless. The values were there, but he definitely needed his spiritual priorities rearranged.

As weeks went by, their differences in lifestyle began to weigh heavily upon Milton. He knew his bond with God was broken, but for whatever reason, his heart was stubborn and resistant to the tug of God. Changes had to be made in his life, and he could perceive his companionship with Ruth was not advancing her faith in Christ. One evening he called her and explained how he felt. Would she meet him Sunday morning at the church so she could return his ring? When Ruth met Milton, she saw a very different young man. He looked so beaten and distraught, she hardly recognized this as the same confident person she had been dating. There wasn't much to say. Reluctantly, Ruth took off his ring and put it back into Milton's hands. It would be some time before he called again.

It was very difficult for Ruth to think this was the end of their relationship. One of her favorite verses from Psalm 139 she had paraphrased to read,

"Formed in the womb and called to be a pastor's wife." That this pastor could be Milton was more than a fleeting thought for Ruth. She found ways to look for him around the campus. She could, unobtrusively, observe him when the band was practicing their marches. Occasionally she would spot him delivering a telegram on his bicycle. Her heart would race as her tears came. But God wanted to deepen her personal dedication to Christ, not simply confirm her desires for the man who would fulfill her dreams.

It was through Ruth's sisters that a new level of consecration was made. Together, the girls made a vow they would not date young men who did not have a passion for Christ. Once that commitment was made, a great load lifted from Ruth's heart.

The testing of that promise was not long coming. Milton's cousin Jack came to town, and the two boys decided to drop in on the Phair girls and see if they would like to go for a drive. Ruth's hair had been washed and was drying in her curlers. She apologized for the situation, but said they really couldn't go. She felt relieved after the boys left. Her newly made consecration meant everything to her, and there was an inner conviction that God was working everything out for His glory.

Like any normal collegian, Milton was as full of nonsense as any of them. For entertainment, he and his friends got a store mannequin and created an elaborate drama, which they worked to perfection on Willamette Street in downtown Eugene. The second Saturday night show at the Mayflower Theater ended around 9:30 pm. The boys had a cap pistol, and as they drove by the front of the emptying theater, two or three shots from the pistol burst out, and the dressed-up mannequin was rolled out of the car into the gutter as the boys sped off. After the streets cleared, one of the guys was assigned to pick up the dirtied mannequin. As much fun as Milton seemed to be having, there was soberness in his spirit as he grew more aware of the eternal nature of the conflict brewing within him.

No longer was there a good reason to attend the preaching part of the Sunday night service. A young lady he had met from the Methodist church would often pick him up at Lighthouse Temple after the orchestra was done. They would enjoy the rest of the evening before she took him home. He continually evaluated her in light of Ruth, and she certainly didn't measure up to that great redhead.

One evening when he was on the dance floor with a girl, he heard within his heart a simple, but clear message, "Milton, you are made for better things than this." That clear call he had received as a twelve-year-old boy, but now so distant, suddenly sprang to life again. He longed for the unmistakable purity of heart he experienced when he was first saved.

It had been almost a year since he and Ruth had broken off their relationship. Conviction was so strong upon him, he feared to cross a street. He knew if he were struck by a car and killed, he would not be resting at peace with Jesus. At corners, he would carefully look both ways, then dash across the street.

As most students do, he always looked for a way to make a few extra dollars. One of his friends knew of a job as an assistant to the bartender at a country club. Milton applied and was hired. He had conveniently not told his mother about this, but she became informed of this new job and where it was located. One evening as the bar was closing, Myra drove up and asked an employee to send Milton out. When Milton neared his mother's car, she rolled down the window and tersely said, "Milton, I never thought I would ever be ashamed of you, but I am!" With that, she rolled up the window and drove away, leaving her son cut to the core.

He finally got fed up with his own indecisiveness. The world hadn't shown anything of lasting value to him. He was sick of having an appearance of religion without really walking with Christ...the phony lifestyle he had been embracing for years now.

In the spring of 1941, he finalized his decision to act, got dressed up and went to the morning service at Lighthouse Temple. The service had been dismissed when Milton walked in. Since a lot of the young college students knew him, he talked informally with them for a while, then blurted out his announcement, "I'm going to come back to church tonight and give my heart to the Lord!" The pronouncement stunned his young friends, but they knew one young lady who would certainly welcome the news. Ruth was overjoyed, and knew what she needed to do. Pray!

That evening, instead of going to the evangelistic service, Ruth stationed herself in the prayer room and began to intercede for Milton. As the service went on, Milton could not concentrate on the message. He was anxiously awaiting the altar call so he could get this awful load off his soul and make his heart right before God. Finally the preaching stopped, and Pastor Fulton began the altar call. A song was sung, and then Pastor continued talking! Milton thought, "Maybe he has forgotten all about an altar call tonight."

Since things weren't moving fast enough, Milton slid out into the aisle and down toward the front where he slipped in between two pews. As he knelt there with the elderly Mr. Crook praying beside him, he began crying out to God for forgiveness. Milton's prayers were not short or quiet as the inner turmoil of his heart gushed out in cries of repentance. Not caring who might be listening, Milton sincerely wanted to get his heart right with God.

When the service was dismissed, a number of people began coming to the prayer room where Ruth was stationed. She knew if Milton said he was coming to give his heart to the Lord, he would be there. Asking one of her friends what all the commotion was out in the sanctuary, she was told Milton was on his knees crying out to God. Ruth was ecstatic!

Milton certainly was cleansed by the Lord that night. He had gone to church for one specific purpose…to get right with God, and it was done! Those wonderful promises in Scripture about God's love and continual faithfulness had been planted in fertile soil. It was a habit of his life that if something was worth doing, it was worth doing with all his might. Now that he was washed from his sins and

Christ reigned supreme in his heart, he was determined to follow Him wholeheartedly.

* * *

Chapter Three

Beginning Afresh

"The Lord will fulfill his purpose for me."
Psalm 138:8

Where was Milton? No one doubted his sincerity that Sunday evening at Lighthouse Temple. His repentance and joy in being reclaimed by Christ was evident to everyone. But where was he? It had been two weeks and he hadn't been seen by anyone around the church. It was as though he had dropped off the end of the earth.

Now that he was a new man in Christ, Milton realized he had to make things right from his past. His mother had trained him carefully in honesty. If he wronged anyone, he must apologize. With these motivations, he braced himself for the difficult task. The music he had permanently borrowed from the University must be returned. Milton explained to the professor that he had given his heart to Christ.

Those he had wronged must know of the inner transformation.

He and his buddies used to meet on weekends in the basement of a downtown office building for drinking and having a good time. One of the persons operated the elevator and could get access to the building for their parties. Following his salvation, Milton showed up at their regular get-together to spend the evening sharing his newfound faith. He didn't put them down for their life's choices; he simply told each of them how the Lord had transformed his life. As he left his buddies, he felt his need to tell them he was unable to continue his friendship with them. Thus, a line of demarcation between his old life and his new was begun.

For a full two weeks, Milton went about burning bridges to his past worldly life. The girl who regularly picked him up on Sunday evenings heard a full account of how Christ had forgiven him, setting his life on a right course. Nothing was going to prevent him from possessing a clean conscience before God and man. Turning back to the worldly life he had been living for the past eight years was not an option. The entire motivation of his life now was "I will never look back! My life belongs one hundred percent to Jesus Christ!"

The radiant beauty of that redhead he had dated a year ago was never far from Milton's mind. He felt she may still be interested in him, but he wanted to make a statement, showing her she was very special to him. What could he do?

It was late spring, and the city was alive with anticipation for the Trail to the Rail pageant at the fairgrounds. It was the biggest event in Eugene and only came around every four years. The town created a huge re-enactment of a historical event based upon the Oregon Trail expeditions and the founding of the state. There were covered wagons, Indian fights, early settlements and exploration—all woven together by original narration.

He made the phone call to Ruth, asking her for the date. Would she go? Nothing could hold her back! Her sisters got the best of their clothes together for a smashing outfit. Milton scraped up a huge sum of money for the best tickets he probably could not afford…equivalent to front-row box seats. When the day arrived, the reunited couple had a marvelous time. It set the stage for a courtship which was both exciting and romantic. Meanwhile, career decisions had to be made.

Milton had a year and a half invested at the University of Oregon, but he didn't see how continuing there would further prepare him for the Lord's work. God's call on his life was urgent. He investigated the two-year program offered by Bible Standard Training School and felt that was where God wanted him. Though small, the school had been born in the revival fires of its host church, Lighthouse Temple. Milton had great respect for E.J. Fulton, president of the college and church pastor.

Opening its doors in January of 1925, with twelve students, Bible Standard Training School had developed a viable Bible and ministry program for its young leaders. It was the west coast training institution of Open Bible Standard Churches. Harold Powers was called from his position at the Open Bible Institute in Des Moines, Iowa, to serve as lead teacher and academic dean. His influence is legendary.

As Milton prepared his heart and mind for school, he found work where he could, and spent all extra time possible with Ruth. He loved to be in the Phair home. The warm, friendly spirit of Ethel Phair and her daughters, and Bill's arrival home from work, made him comfortable. Not only was the family alive in the Lord, they also exuded an air of acceptance and love. The contrast could not be greater between this hospitable home and the strict, unemotional one in which he was raised.

Ethel often busied herself in the kitchen making pastries or special dishes, with Milton shadowing her. When she stood still long enough, he could tie her apron strings in some pretty complex knots. She was a good sport, putting up with his teasing. Having a young man around was a refreshing addition to the six-woman household.

Bible school was everything he expected, and more. Harold Powers' teaching and passion began building godly habits and strength into his spiritual life. He could see the Bible as not simply a roadmap to follow, but the very Word of God. It must be given first place in the life of every person serious about discipleship. Key verses and sections needed to be committed to memory. As Mr. Powers taught his classes, Milton often heard him say, "There is only one Book you have to know, and you must fill your mind, heart, and soul with its message!"

In addition to classes, where Milton always received excellent marks, he was prominent in activities of the school. He served as editor of the annual, was a member of student evangelism and music teams, and found time to have fun with creative writing. He illustrated some of the writing for the school paper with original cartoons. Most of the faculty and students got a kick out of them, but there were some negative reactions when certain teachers saw themselves caricatured by the Stewart pen.

In the winter months, when the rains came pouring down and the basement schoolrooms flooded, Milton and Gil Henderson were assigned the responsibility of blocking up the valuables of the school. They hopped on their bicycles and rode through the encroaching waters, down the hallway to the library where the piano and valuable books had to be elevated above water level. Once the basement was pumped dry, the boys removed the blocks, and classes were ready again.

Meanwhile, Ruth was in her senior year at Springfield High School. Fellow students soon recognized she had made a serious commitment, that year, to follow Christ. In her literature class she was given the assignment to write about her projected life after high school. She handed in a well-written essay on the life of a pastor's wife. The "A" she received on the paper must have been for mechanics, because, as she later admitted, she certainly didn't know what lay ahead of her as a pastor's wife.

That spring, Ruth began practicing hard for her performance in the state music competition. Mr. Roach graciously loaned her his very expensive violin and bow for this special occasion. She had her violin concerto thoroughly memorized when she confidently walked onto the stage facing the judges seated on the front row. As she moved through her piece, she realized the bowstrings on her borrowed instrument had not been completely tightened. The most difficult passage was coming up, and she knew it would be impossible to play it properly without tightening the strings.

She stopped playing, tightened the bowstrings, and continued. The judges were writing furiously. She knew it would cost her dearly, but she wanted to play the passage with the zest it was meant to have. Although her critiques and comments were great, she was only given a third-level finish. It had been a brief stumble, but Ruth did not let it discourage her from giving her musical talents to the Lord. To this day, she has blessed countless people through her anointed ministry on the violin. "Ruth is a more accomplished violinist than I am a cornet player," Milton has often testified.

Ruth and Milton had started dating again the summer before he started Bible school. It was obvious they were very fond of each other, and Milton was quite free in telling his friends he was going to marry her. The problem was, Ruth wasn't being told.

As fall arrived, he spent as much time as he could spare with Ruth. Getting to and from her house in Springfield posed a big problem. He used the buses most of the time, but as young lovers know, sometimes the time goes whistling by, and the last bus has left. What then? It was a long walk from east Springfield back to his apartment and roommate, Harold. When he thought far enough ahead, he would sometimes lean on Harold to drive him to the Phair home, hang around until just before curfew, then take him home.

Milton may have been a bit unaware of the passing of time, but Ruth wasn't. She had heard from her friends around church that Milton really was in love with her, but she hadn't heard it from him. Nobody likes to be prodded, but it seemed necessary to his roommate Harold that he speak up. "Hey, Milt," he said one day that fall, "don't you realize Ruth is pretty crazy about you? You need to get on the ball and do something about it!"

Those in Bible school had many reason to be aware of the relationship. Monday mornings when disciplinary notices were announced, too often Milton would have been charged with arriving home after curfew, and it wasn't because of his work schedule. In fact, on several occasions, Mr. Powers would "happen" to be driving around late and see Milton out walking. Milton would get into his car and, without a word being spoken between them, Mr. Powers would drive him to his apartment. Even the Bible college president and church pastor, E.J. Fulton gave him a "late" ride home. He had to be written up, but Milton's priorities remained: Ruth first, school second.

One evening during that winter, Milton and Ruth were visiting on the front porch of her home. Ruth was getting a bit exasperated about not having a firm proposal from him, so she decided to help him out. "Milton," she said, "you know, I don't want to be just another one of your girl friends!"

It stung him a bit, because it reminded him of the girl from the Methodist church choir who picked him up after orchestra at church. Compared to Ruth, she meant nothing. Besides, he hadn't seen or thought about her since he told her he had committed his life to Christ.

Finally, he turned to Ruth and blurted, "Don't you know I am in love with you and want to marry you?" It wasn't the poetic script he might have chosen if the proposal had been planned, but it did the job just fine for Ruth. There wasn't a big response from her, because about then, Ruth's mom stuck her head out the front door and announced it was getting a bit late. With their future committed to each other, now the couple could start making some plans.

Tuition was a regular monthly bill, and Milton's part-time work barely kept him current. As he and Ruth looked for rings, he knew it would be tough to buy a set on his income. They finally settled on a nice small set and purchased it using his next month's tuition money. It took a while to catch up with tuition, but the sacrifice made to purchase the symbols of the promised future marriage to the love of his life was worth it.

One evening late that spring, the young couple let the time get away from them. After it was too late, they realized Milton had missed the last bus. He was staying with his folks, way out on River Road ten miles away. They said their last good-byes, and Milton took off. Even at a fast pace, it would be close to three hours before he arrived home. Dead tired, but still walking, he slipped into sleep mode. His collision with the telephone pole was pretty ugly. It knocked him down and bruised up his face a bit. At least he wouldn't get called on the carpet for breaking school curfew.

Ruth's Uncle William tried to throw a curve ball into Milton's reputation. He and his wife had lived next door to the McDowells, in Dillard, when Milton was in elementary school. William was quite a self-righteous Christian and very opinionated. Since he had several times observed drinking in the McDowell home, he felt anyone who came from such an environment would certainly not be worthy of associating with the Phairs. When he heard Milton was courting one of the girls, he gave his brother the blunt message, "Tell your daughters not to have anything to do with that man. He's nothing but bad news."

Milton was not conscious of any wariness Ruth's parents had toward him, but this message from a family member did put them on notice. What they were observing in Milton, however, was unpretentious sincerity and honesty. He may have been young in his faith, but his zeal for the Lord was real. They resolved to maintain their confidence in him.

There was a lot for Milton to think about in the spring of '42. Japan had bombed Pearl Harbor in December, and America was involved in World War II on both the Pacific and Atlantic fronts. Able-bodied men across the country were enlisting in the armed forces. He was engaged to be married, with no definite date set. The Bible school rules stated enrolled students were not allowed to marry during the school year. This seemed a disappointment to Ruth and Milton. Glenn Doney, one of his classmates, was planning to preach summer revival meetings in the Midwest. Milton was invited to be in charge of music at these revivals. He had already memorized Proverbs 3:5-6: "Trust in the Lord with all your heart and lean not on your own understanding; in all your ways acknowledge him, and he will make your paths straight." He was confident God would clarify His will to him.

Although he was young in the Lord, two firm convictions stayed with him through life: He knew Christ had called him to preach the Gospel, and he knew God's Word was true from cover to cover. He found a private place in the school library to make his regular prayer closet, more secluded than the church prayer room on the main level. One evening, as he knelt there alone, he felt two hands around his neck beginning to choke the life from him. Panic stricken, he jumped to his feet, only to find the room empty. He quickly ran out the door, up the steps and out into the night. It would not be the last time the devil attacked Milton in a physical manner, but the event only served to solidify his confidence in the reality of his faith in Christ.

He and Ruth felt the evangelism experience in the Midwest would be a valuable open door. Glenn's father pastored a church in Denver and arranged for a recently purchased tent to be taken to the small country town of Phillipsburg, Kansas. The two beginning evangelists set up the tent, complete with center and side posts, ropes and stakes. Such a sight in a small town was not uncommon, and the home folks knew they were going to have revival meetings.

The afternoon before the evening services were to begin, the weather got hot and humid. Glenn left the hotel where they were staying to prepare for the meeting on site. Milton stayed behind to pray. Due to the suffocating heat, he opened a window, buried his head between the mattresses and began praying. Feeling drops of rain on his backside, he turned around and stared into the face of a severe storm. Out of the eerie afternoon darkness, wind was blowing horizontal rain right through his window.

Grabbing his tie, he left the hotel and fought his way down the windswept street until he arrived at their wildly flapping tent. This wasn't simply another storm; it was a Midwest tornado. There in the middle of the tent was Glenn, hanging onto the center post for dear life, his wind-swept body straight out from the ground. Milton could see red stains all over Glenn's white shirt. Rushing to him, he quickly saw Glenn's red tie had gotten wet and bled all over the shirt. The two friends helped each other outside; then began the task of attempting to salvage their tent. They found an axe, which they used to cut the ropes and bring the flapping canvas down. It was too late. What remained of the tent was unsalvageable for public use. A couple of days later, a truck picked up the leftovers and took them to another town for reclamation.

Milton and Glenn felt fortunate, escaping with their lives. The tornadoes that summer in Kansas were particularly deadly. After canceling meetings, Glenn accepted an invitation to preach at a nearby church, and Milton returned to Denver, where he joined an evangelist as the song leader and soloist.

Milton and Ruth kept in touch through letters and an occasional care package sent from Eugene. One of his packages contained half a dozen apron strings, with a note from Ethel Phair, "Don't lose your touch tying knots, Milton!" Through the summer, Ruth was much in prayer about God's timing for their marriage, but a letter Milton received from another source diverted their attention.

Uncle Sam wrote Milton, telling him to report to Leavenworth, Kansas, for induction into the armed forces. When he arrived, all recruits were given a thorough physical and mental exam. He passed most of the basics with flying colors, and was nearly ready for induction, when an officer called him aside. "Milton, I want you to talk with the examination doctor."

When the doctor arrived, he told Milton of his concern about his eyes, and what the exam had revealed. He then asked for Milton's papers. Across the top of the letterhead he stamped in red "Medical Disqualification." Summer was nearly over as he boarded the train for his ride back to Denver.

As Ruth prayed, she felt a growing conviction that she and Milton should be married before school began in the fall. Milton agreed. Since he would be arriving home on the weekend, and school started Wednesday, there was no time to waste. Monday morning, borrowing $3.50 from a friend, he and Ruth went to the courthouse to purchase their marriage license. He then called Lighthouse Temple to talk with Pastor E.J. Fulton. Would he be willing to marry them on Tuesday, prior to the evening service?

It had not escaped Pastor Fulton that school was beginning on Wednesday morning. Nothing would make this couple happier than starting off this new school year married, and in the good graces of the Bible school. His positive answer had come to Ruth in prayer several weeks earlier, but the pair was overjoyed when he actually agreed to marry them on such short notice. No time to plan for a big church wedding for them.

When Tuesday evening arrived, two close friends, Willyla Bushnell of the Bible school faculty, and Warren Moore, a personal friend, stood up for the couple in Fulton's office. The ceremony was short and sweet, and the happy couple began their married life together on September 29, 1942.

The first week of married life was a whirlwind of activity. Classes opened Wednesday morning.

His ministry ventures of the summer were profitable spiritually, but left him with virtually no money. Job-hunting was his focus, and thankfully, there was an abundance of good jobs available, due to the loss of manpower diverted to the war effort. One of his first jobs was firing the engines in a railroad round house. His Swedish boss was ticked off because he had just lost the last man he had trained to the military. He wasn't at all pleased to go through the same procedures with a new man, so he simply did as little as possible to help Milton learn the ropes. Milton was assigned the graveyard shift, 11:00 p.m. to 7:00 a.m., giving him precious little time before his first class began at school.

One night, he was faced with four huge engines in the round house, at the same time. They all had to be lit, then brought up to 50 pounds of steam pressure. To do this, Milton had to turn on each atomizer, turn on the blower, light a wad of waste, and throw the wad into the fire to ignite each engine. His disgruntled, black-bearded boss wasn't about to help this young railroad recruit. All the big Swede seemed good for was a pound of criticism for every ounce of instruction. When Milton threw in the lit waste on the largest of the four engines, the fire blew off into the pit. Flames shot up all around the cabin of the engine. The old Swede's only action was to stand outside his office yelling, cursing and shouting at the novice.

It took awhile, but somehow Milton was able to get the fire under control. All the engines were safely moved, with no lasting damage observed. He was never so happy to see 7:00 a.m. in his life. That afternoon, when he was sleeping, he was sure the Lord spoke to him saying, "Get out of there!" It was one nudge from the Lord he was more than happy to obey.

It didn't take him long to land a job selling shoes with J.C. Penney. For a young outgoing man who enjoyed dressing his best, the job was a good fit. It lasted through his graduation. Ruth's parents helped them by butchering a pig and sharing the meat. Money was tight, but God was good, and married life was oh, so wonderful.

Ruth enrolled in school, taking several academic and practical classes. She loved her newfound friends at BSTI. To help with expenses, she advertised violin lessons for sale. Four young students came under her tutelage, bringing in $1.00 each, per week. The school let her use a room in its basement for the lessons.

During a missionary service, a special offering was taken. Ruth's heart was touched, and she gave all her lesson money to the missionary cause. After the service, she and Milton talked about the service and found he had done the same thing. Each was counting on the other's money for the week ahead, and now they were broke. Before they left for home that evening, someone handed them a wad of money, and smiled. They counted it, and discovered it was double what they had given toward the missionary cause.

Milton's final year at Bible Standard Training Institute flew by in a blur of activity. There was an obvious anointing upon Milton's life, whether he was preaching the Gospel or playing his cornet. The effectiveness of his ministry seemed to more than double when joined by Ruth. Not only could she play the violin like a professional, she and Milton sang inspired duets wherever they were called upon to minister. Ruth believed in God's call upon her husband, and she also knew God had called her to support him and be a safe haven for him through the highs and lows of a minister's life.

As the school year drew to a close and the Stewarts were about to begin their first ministry, they were blessed in a special way by Ruth's dad, Bill Phair. Taking Milton aside one day, Mr. Phair told him plainly, "Milton, we love you. When I was first saved, I felt God's call upon my life, to preach the Gospel. I didn't follow that call, but I believe you are now doing exactly what God called me to do so many years ago. You can count on us to be praying for you and Ruth." Those were invaluable words to the young couple.

* * *

Chapter Four

Launching a Ministry

*"...for I am compelled to preach. Woe to me
if I do not preach the gospel!"*
1 Corinthians 9:16

Powers, Oregon

As Milton was finishing Bible school, he and
Ruth knew God had called them into ministry.
When they heard there was an opening at Powers,
Oregon, they immediately made themselves available. Having lived there during his freshman year of
high school with his mother and stepfather, Milton
was returning to a community he knew. The Open
Bible Church had only a handful of people, but it
was a start, and he would be in familiar territory. The
Powers church had been born as an outgrowth of the
1920s revivals in Eugene, and had the distinction

of being the home of the Bible institute's first two students, Senethea Meyer and Jae Bushnell.

That first summer of ministry for Milton and Ruth started with a bang. They invited Eva and Frieda Surls, musical sisters who also effectively ministered the Word, to hold a tent-revival meeting in Powers over a ten-day span in August. The revival meetings were well attended. The folks in Powers got a good introduction to the Gospel and the new preacher at the Open Bible Church. Ruth had gone to Springfield to live with her folks as she awaited the delivery of their first child. Pam was born on August 15th, 1943, and due to the revival meetings, it was ten days before Milton could get free to see his first-born. When the revival concluded, he made the trip to Eugene, entered the hospital, and picked up his daughter. He thought he had never seen anything so beautiful in his life. He held his baby almost continually, reveling in God's gift of life to Ruth and him. A couple of days later they drove back to their sparse home in Powers. It consisted of two and a half rooms in the back of the church, with the kitchen serving as Pam's bedroom.

Milton's old Christian Church, where he had attended as a high school freshman, had suffered a fire and had no building of its own. The congregation had found temporary space for their services in the local community building. When they realized the new pastor at the Open Bible Church was their former boy, the whole Christian Church congregation decided to attend Milton's first church and support "one of their own." Even though the church was nearly filled, there was no sense of Christian camaraderie between the Pentecostals and those of the Christian Church. The Open Bible Church people would have nothing to do with the visitors, and this divisiveness became apparent in nearly everything Stewarts attempted to do for the Gospel's sake.

A pregnant teen-aged girl was injured badly when she jumped off a bridge in an apparent suicide attempt. The Stewarts called on her, and she responded by coming to church. When the altar call was given, she went forward and knelt. No one in the church was willing to pray with her, so Stewarts led her to the Lord. She later lost her baby, but dedicated her life to Christ, and eventually enrolled at Eugene Bible College.

Among the young people he influenced were members of the Boy Scout troop he led. Milton would often play football with them on the front lawn of the church. Through his interaction with these boys, several had come to Christ. However, they incurred the wrath of the board for messing up the church's lawn. Milton was pretty disgusted with their lack of vision and told his board members, "A young boy's soul is a lot more important than this grass on the front lawn."

It wasn't his only confrontation with the board, as he was quite outspoken. Later in life, he shuddered to think how brash he really was at times. One evening the board was in prayer when one of the more spiteful members came in late. As she approached the others, she grumbled aloud, "I felt the devil as soon as I came in here." Milton replied, "No wonder you did; you brought him with you!"

The Stewarts had ministered in Powers for nine months when they received an invitation to serve as assistant pastors in music at a Midwest church.

Sioux Falls, South Dakota

William Dirks was the church's senior pastor and director of a well-received radio ministry. Ruth and Milton were put in charge of all church music, including the radio ministry. They sang duets, played their instruments, and served together as treasurers of the church. Part of their radio ministry was visiting many churches within the region of their radio coverage. One embarrassing evening was especially memorable.

Ruth and Milton were singing in a Covenant Church with very poor lighting. In the middle of their duet, Milton could no longer read the music, so he began making up the words. Ruth was so taken off guard she burst into tears. The couple found a way to end the song, then quickly left the platform...a most humbling experience.

From their earliest days in ministry, God used their musical talents to open up people to the Gospel and communicate the message of Jesus. With faces lifted toward heaven, they played and sang "as unto the Lord" with skill and anointing. As gifted as they were, the call of God upon Milton to preach the Gospel was predominate, and he itched to get back into the pulpit and develop as a minister of the Good News.

Riverton, Wyoming

Open Bible Churches' headquarters reported a group in Riverton, Wyoming, needed a pastor. The church had no building, but OBC gave the Stewarts $100 and their bus fare, so the challenge was accepted. Upon arrival in town, the young couple, with their baby girl, first stayed in a small cabin. A few weeks later, a member of their new congregation invited them to occupy one side of his duplex, rent-free. This agreement lasted for the two years of their Riverton ministry.

After the couple found and rented a meeting hall in the basement of the Franklin Store, a carpenter was hired to build a pulpit and altar rail for the church. Since the Veterans of Foreign Wars also used the space on Saturday nights for social events, Milton arrived early Sunday morning to sweep out the hall, pick up cigar and cigarette butts, and get things cleaned up for the morning service.

As was their custom wherever they ministered, the Stewarts held street meetings in Riverton. With Milton on his cornet and Ruth playing her violin, quite a crowd would gather for singing and music. Most of them stayed for the preaching. There were times when as many a 200 people gathered around the Stewarts as they shared the Gospel in music and preaching on the streets this frontier town.

Milton was hungry for more of the Lord and went through quite a period of testing in Riverton. Ruth prayed earnestly for her husband. She had received the baptism in the Spirit during her time at Bible school, but Milton had not yet received. He seriously began questioning his call to preach, and his capability to earn a living in any other profession. His hunger for God's blessing in his life bordered on obsession. He was zealous for anything that would stimulate him spiritually. Finding inspirational reading for both mind and soul in Riverton, Wyoming, seemed absurd, but God gave him his heart's desire.

An elderly neighbor living around the corner from Stewarts had attended the training school led by Charles Haddon Spurgeon of England. He had purchased copies of the many volumes written by Spurgeon. Since this gentleman knew Spurgeon personally, all his books were autographed by the famous preacher. Eagerly, Milton asked him if he could ever read any of them. The gentleman responded, "Yes, but this is how we will do it. You come and check out one of his books. You must return it within one week. Then you may check out another." With the conditions agreed upon, Milton eagerly read every Spurgeon book in the gentleman's library before he left town. What a gold mine!

As the church salary was not enough to support the Stewart family, Milton found a job driving truck for an oil company. Without adequate training on the mechanics of his truck and the dangers inherent in working with natural gas and crude oil, Milton could have lost his life one afternoon while filling his truck tank. Since he did not fully understand the safety procedures to observe while filling, Milton stationed himself atop the tank. He simply meant to shut off and remove the hose before the tank was filled, but didn't realize he was breathing the toxic natural gas fumes until they nearly rendered him unconscious. Thoroughly frightened from the experience, he turned in his resignation and found a job at the local Safeway store.

In April of their first spring in Riverton, Ruth was pregnant with her second daughter, Pat. As time for the birth neared, Riverton got 18 inches of late snow, and the doctor scheduled for the delivery could not get to the hospital. With Ruth hospitalized and no doctor available, the couple prayed mightily. Then she began her hard labor. A few minutes later, assisted by Dr. Daddy, Pat was born. It was April 8th, 1945.

One day the city council called the area pastors to attend a meeting of general community interest. Milton found the council was going to sponsor a dance for their high school students and wanted a minister to oversee the event. He answered in a manner he later felt was too outspoken, "I don't believe in modern dancing," he stated, "and I am not willing to be a sponsor or participate in any way. My conscience will not allow me to do it."

The Nazarene pastor was angered at his reply, but the city manager cornered him on his way out with a question that opened many doors for the young preacher. "Say, Milton, do you ever give lessons on the horn?" he asked. After a brief talk, it was decided Milton would instruct his son on the instrument.

In a few weeks, he was teaching beginning lessons to four or five high school students on such varied instruments as the trumpet, clarinet, baritone, trombone and saxophone. He went to the music store, purchased books for each horn, and keeping about two lessons ahead of his students, led them through beginning steps on their instruments.

The parents of Milton's instrumental students could see what an outstanding job he was accomplishing with their kids. When the high school band teacher had to go on leave, due to illness, it seemed natural to recommend Milton as his substitute. The students responded enthusiastically.

Later that spring, the city fathers made him an offer very hard to refuse: If he would go back to college and get teaching credentials in music, they would pay for all his schooling, and hire him as the full-time music director at the school. This certainly was an answer to the nagging question of his worth in the job market. Although buoyed by their confidence in his ability to teach their children, he could not turn his back on God's call to preach the Gospel. Reluctantly, he turned down their generous offer. Later, he was asked to direct the volunteer Riverton town band. What a joy! His love of young people and of band music brought great satisfaction throughout that year.

Thornton, Washington

The Stewarts came back to Eugene to visit Ruth's parents and meet with E.J. Fulton, their regional superintendent. Informed that OBC was going to close the church in the small farming community of Thornton, WA, south of Spokane, Milton and Ruth volunteered to go there and trust God to bless their efforts. Their one-year ministry in Thornton proved fruitful.

The house they lived in was almost perfectly square, having four rooms: a living room, two bedrooms and a kitchen. The outhouse in the back, of course, was the bathroom. The exterior of the house had never been painted, and rather than a sidewalk, it had two planks leading from the front porch to the driveway. The pastor preceding Stewarts had applied wallpaper to all interior walls, laid linoleum on all floors, and done a makeshift job of wiring the house. That's where there were serious problems. Being a rural community, there had been no enforcement of the wiring codes, and the fixer-upper job was far from complete. To turn lights on and off, they had to screw and unscrew the light bulbs. Stewarts were able to complete the wiring with wall switches and an up-to-code standard. Stewarts didn't plan to become home remodelers, but that seemed to be included in this package.

Again, the income from the church wasn't suffi-cient to support the Stewart family, and before Milton could get supplemental work, even food was a needy item. They remember sitting around the table with empty plates in front of them, praying for God to meet their needs. The doorbell rang; the family found two large boxes of food on the front porch, provided by God via the generous people of the town. Bobbi Jo's birth was one more manifestation of God's blessing on their lives. Now Ruth could begin thinking about arranging trio music for her daughters.

Plunging into their work with enthusiasm and prayer, they began to see the Lord bless. As was his practice, Milton went around town and met all the other local pastors. He made a friend of the Methodist pastor, and after discussing the various needs of their churches and the community, the men decided to join forces for one strong Sunday evening service to include both congregations. As planned, Milton would preach one Sunday evening at the Methodist church, and the next week the Methodist pastor would preach at the Open Bible Church. Nobody could have anticipated the results of this arrangement.

There was a great move of God in the area, and on many occasions the church was packed for the service. All four Methodist board members got saved and left the church to be under the ministry of the Stewarts. The Methodist organist, who was in her mid-seventies, had served her church for over thirty years. While visiting in her home, Milton and Ruth asked her if she had ever asked Jesus Christ to forgive her sins and come into her heart as personal Savior and Lord. She couldn't remember this happening to her, so Milton led her in a sinner's prayer. When they finished, she gasped, "I never knew it was possible to feel like this!"

Of the 25 high school students in town, all but one was a part of the youth group in the Open Bible Church. It was not Milton's intention to steal church members, but when people who belong to a "social-gospel" church get genuinely converted and want to attend a different church for biblical nourishment, how can they be turned away?

Ralph Henning was a Thornton wheat farmer with approximately 1,500 acres under cultivation. Ralph was saved, along with his family, but decided to stay in the Methodist church. Milton needed to earn some extra money for his family, so he drove truck for Mr. Henning during harvest. From early morning until setting sun, he would follow the combine, load his truck with grain, and drive to the local elevator where he dumped the load. Going back to the fields, the process was repeated until the end of the day. The hours and diligence that went into harvesting wheat became a lasting memory and illustration of the Gospel for Milton. He also had an insatiable hunger and thirst to be used in his Father's great harvest of souls. And all the more critical; he was working with a spiritually perishable crop.

Milton's musical ability, ardent preaching, and enthusiasm for Christ opened many doors. He and his wife were in demand at Youth for Christ rallies as far away as Lewiston, Idaho. Some closer churches asked him to come hold revival meetings in their communities. Milton accepted an invitation from a nearby Assembly of God pastor and began a revival meeting at his church. Convinced as he was that God had called him to preach, he also felt inferior because God had not yet baptized him in the Holy Spirit.

In preparation for the evening revival service, Milton spent much time alone at the church in prayer. While praying one afternoon, he literally felt flames shooting up his back. Jumping up wildly, he twisted around to see if he was on fire. After a few moments, he came to the conclusion it was an attack of the enemy. He began a serious examination of his heart and came to an awkward decision. In his conscience, he felt hypocritical to be preaching to a Pentecostal congregation about a life in the Spirit he believed in, but had not fully entered. At Milton's insistence, the pastor canceled the remainder of the revival meetings, and he returned to his church in Thornton.

Martinez, California

The occasion for change came again for Milton and his family. Would he be willing to move to Martinez, California, to pastor the established church there? After prayer, the Stewarts responded with a "Yes" and left Thornton with their belongings in the back seat and on the roof rack of their '35 Ford sedan. Pam and Pat sat high up on the baggage with their heads snuggled against the roof; Bobbi Jo was in Ruth's arms.

As they were leaving Oakridge on their way over the Cascade Mountains, Milton and Ruth decided to stop and have a time of prayer, committing their trip and their lives to the Lord. They had just pulled off the road when brakes screeched, and a large car hit their back left fender, nearly tearing it off. The lady had apparently gone to sleep at the wheel when she veered into the Stewarts' car. Milton turned his Ford around, and back to Oakridge they went to see what could be done for repairs. The auto repairman had no parts; the Stewarts had no money, so Milton talked him into cutting off the whole fender. This done, they got back on the road.

Excitement mounted as they were coming through the Siskiyou Mountains, approaching beautiful Mount Shasta. They parked the car to take a better look and snap some pictures. Milton had to climb on top of the car to get into the rack for the camera. While scrambling around, he stuck his foot through the back window, glass going everywhere. The next hour was spent removing jagged glass from the window frame and picking up all the shards they could find on their luggage and household goods in the back seat. One great benefit for the girls—they now could wave and put on a show for those cars following them down Highway 99 toward Martinez.

Arriving at their destination, the Stewarts followed directions to the parsonage, which was toward the bottom of a fairly steep hill. Milton drove down the driveway, parked in front of the garage, set the mechanical emergency brake, and started to unload. Then it happened. The brakes failed, and the car began moving forward, crashing into the garage doors, battering them badly. They opened the damaged doors and Milton thought he'd get the Ford into the garage. Easing it forward, he realized too late there wasn't enough clearance for their belongings stored in the rack on the roof. The ensuing collision with the garage-door header smashed the rack through the roof of their car. They were finally home, but when Sunday came, Ruth would not let Milton park their beat-up car within two blocks of the church.

Since Milton was now salaried and no longer had to provide work outside the church to support his growing family, he devoted himself full-time to the ministry. He had now been preaching for over four years and had yet to receive the baptism in the Holy Spirit. Everywhere he went he engaged other pastors in discussions on the filling of the Holy Spirit. He listened intently to a variety of explanations:

"You received the Holy Spirit when you were saved."

"The baptism in the Holy Spirit is an experience of 'entire sanctification' whereby God does a work of holiness in you, giving you freedom from the carnal nature."

"The gift of the Holy Spirit is subsequent to salvation and is given to empower the believer for a life of service, witnessing, and holiness."

He read books on the subject, but nothing satisfied him, except what he saw in God's Word. The influence of his teachers and early pastors in Eugene gave him hope this "baptism" was ready and available for him. He could see the baptism in the Holy Spirit made an essential difference in the lives of the leadership in the early church of the book of Acts. And it certainly seemed to be an event separate from salvation. Those receiving this baptism were also exercising gifts of the Holy Spirit: miracles, healings, signs and wonders all followed the ministry of many who were filled. If it happened then, and "Jesus Christ was the same, yesterday, today and forever," why couldn't we expect the same today? He was badgered by the questions of why he hadn't yet been filled, and what might be wrong with him. His conclusion? He wasn't good enough to be trusted with this marvelous gift.

Early in his ministry in Martinez, he made a decision to seek the Lord in prayer with the same dedication his wheat-farming friend, Mr. Henning, had exhibited in bringing in his harvest in Thornton. He vowed, "I'll spend as much time seeking God and preparing myself for ministry as I did getting in the harvest for Mr. Henning!" This meant he got up every day at daybreak and went to the church for prayer and time in the Word. He sought God, especially for His power and presence. This he would do from the early morning hours until early afternoon, or often into the evening. Several other local ministers joined Milton at various times during this spiritual quest.

On a Wednesday morning in 1948, Milton had been praying with a women's group. After they were dismissed, he was left alone. Without opening his Bible, God spoke verses from Colossians 1:10-14 into his heart. He had read them often, but had not memorized them. The 12th verse was central to what the Lord breathed into his life, "And joyfully giving thanks to the Father, who has qualified you to share in the inheritance of the saints in the kingdom of light."

The phrase, "who has qualified you," leaped up in his soul as he fully accepted the truth of God's Word. It was Christ himself who had made him, Milton Stewart, worthy of receiving the "full inheritance" of the Father. This certainly included the baptism in the Holy Spirit! It set his inner man free. What a release from the bondage of unworthiness he had been trapped in for years!

With God's presence so near, he asked the question, "What do I do now, Father?" God's answer was very clear: "Just do what my Word says." Milton then realized the verse simply stated he was to "joyfully thank the Father." He lifted his arms and began to praise God. It seemed so easy to thank God for all His goodness, and for the freedom experienced in being made worthy. It took awhile before he realized he was not speaking to God in English, but in other tongues, as the disciples had done in the book of Acts. For the next hour or more, he worshiped the Lord, both in tongues and plain English. He became fully aware of the "streams of living water" (John 7:38) flowing in him, which Jesus called the precious promised Holy Spirit indwelling the believer.

When he got home, Ruth could tell something special had happened to him. They sat down and talked over the incredible release God had given him, and the power he experienced in the presence of God. From her own experience, Ruth explained that after speaking in tongues, he was probably then giving the interpretation in English. This, she pointed out, happened often in the early church and was a part of Paul's teaching in 1 Corinthians 14.

While talking with his wife about the morning experiences, he felt the Spirit might have leaked out. Excusing himself, he went into his daughter's bedroom, got down on his knees and began praying once more. No, he was assured in his spirit this new baptism in the Spirit had not left him. As he walked in God's truth, he learned, with all Spirit-filled Christians, that walking in the Spirit is very much an act of faith, and not dependent upon emotion or feelings. The pouring out of the Holy Spirit on Milton did not stop with that single event. When God gives the gift of the Holy Spirit, He does not take it back. That day absolutely transformed his life. Now that he had walked through the door into the life of the Spirit, he was determined to live in that life, and allow the Holy Spirit to fill and use him daily.

On Sunday morning, Milton was completely undecided about his sermon. The big pulpit Bible was on the lectern, but he had no direction from the Lord. Before he stepped up to speak, the Lord spoke to his heart ever so clearly, "Milton, you just stand up, open that Bible and read." With this oversized Bible opened to Proverbs 2, he read the scripture passage and then, for the next 30 minutes, the message of God gushed out of him. He felt like an observer standing off the platform watching himself act as a conduit for the message God was pouring through him. As abruptly as it started, God's message stopped.

The service closed, but for the next two weeks there was a visitation of the blessing and presence of God never before seen in that church. It was like heaven on earth! Even as people arrived, they were met by a powerful awareness of God's presence. Without direction from the pastor, the congregation worshiped: some kneeling, others lying on the floor, still others simply standing with arms raised in worship to the Lord. It may have looked chaotic to an outsider, but God was doing business in the individual lives of people.

A man brought in a prostitute who needed help. She was led to the front of the church and the Stewarts began leading her to Christ. Her friend became belligerent with Milton as he was sharing the Gospel with her. Milton could see he had to be removed or she likely would not be able to freely respond to the Lord. He asked one of the church's mature believers, Sam McGibney, to take care of this gentleman. Sam took the man by the arm and led him outside the church where he simply told him, "Now, stay here." Turning around, he went back into the church, closing the door behind him. There was no more interference, and the woman was marvelously saved.

Two truck drivers, married to sisters, came to a service with their wives. All four went to the altar, even though they had to walk around and over some church members who were lying on the floor. Not only were they all saved, the men were called by God to preach the Gospel. Years later, Milton met one of them who was pastoring a church in Drain, Oregon. He joyfully told Milton his brother-in-law was also a minister of the Gospel.

Mr. Willer had been a member of the Martinez church for some time. His son Frank, in spite of his cerebral palsy, loved the Lord deeply and served the church as their custodian. Watching Frank dusting the pews during the week moved Milton deeply. In between his dusting, he would pause and pray for the people who would be seated in those pews. Tears would flow down his cheeks as he unburdened his heart to the Lord. Milton could feel the rhythm of his life, "Dust and sweep, pray and weep; dust and sweep, pray and weep." He came to believe God's blessing in that congregation was an answer to Frank's prayers, as much or more than his own.

This special visitation from God affected the congregation deeply. Many had been healed and others filled with the Spirit. Most of those in the church experienced the presence of God in a memorable way that deepened their faith in the living Lord and His Word. The neighbors right across the street from the church were saved. Fifty years later, the children and grandchildren of that family were still serving Christ and attending the church.

Although there were great victories won in Martinez, Ruth and Milton were also to experience significant tests. Ruth began to have some soreness in her breast and felt a hard lump there. It seemed to be growing, and she finally went to the doctor for an exam. He was concerned, and asked her to come back for a biopsy. Before this appointment was arranged, an evangelist, who believed in the working of the Holy Spirit and healing, was invited to the church for meetings. God was moving effectively in the church, and one evening Ruth went forward for prayer. When the evangelist laid his hands on her, the Spirit of the Lord strongly witnessed to her heart. She was confident God had done a miracle in her.

Ruth never made another appointment with her doctor. As the days and weeks went by, she became aware the lump was still present, and it was sore.

At the same time, in her spirit, Ruth knew God had touched her. She would not deny the miracle she received from the Lord that night when she asked for prayer. She told only her husband and her father, Bill Phair, of the battle she was going through. Her father generously offered to pay for any operation she needed, but Ruth was determined to trust God. His answer, as we shall see, was not immediate.

The Lord spoke very vividly to Milton one evening, instructing him to get into his car and God would direct him to a person who was in desperate need of help. He obeyed the Lord and began driving through the neighborhoods, led by God's prompting. As he approached a certain house, the Lord indicated this was where he should to stop and pray for the person inside. He began having a fight with his natural man. How stupid it would be if this were his imagination! He paused in front of the house, thinking if he really were supposed to stop, perhaps the Lord would give him an additional revelation or confirmation of his will.

As he drove on by, his heart was grieved. He turned around and went back. Was this really God, or some wild goose chase going on in his super-spiritual imagination? On past the house he drove, back to the parsonage. He didn't think very much about it until a couple of days later when he picked up the newspaper and read that a distraught young woman had drowned her two children in their bathtub. The article included the street address of her house. His heart sank. It was the very residence the Lord had led him to a few evenings earlier.

In agony of heart, Milton went back to his Lord. He repented of his disobedience and asked God to revive and renew his sensitivities to the leading of the Holy Spirit. He wanted more than ever to be a vessel God could use, trust, and work through. By His grace, God restored the broken man and birthed in his heart a vision of the miraculous acts the Lord was willing to do through His humbled servant. There seemed to be a tenderness in Milton's spirit brought on by that encounter that became a vital part of his person through the rest of his life.

"If we are faithless,
he will remain faithful,
for he cannot disown himself."
2 Timothy 2:13

* * *

Chapter Five

Lewiston and Revival

"...open your eyes and look at the fields!
They are ripe for harvest."
John 4:35

Recruitment to Ministry

Milton loved the challenge of evangelistic work and fully intended to make a permanent move to that type of ministry. He held several series of meetings, which were encouraging in their results, but there was one huge obstacle he kept facing. He did not see how he could be a responsible family man and be away from home for the periods of time it would take to be successful in his evangelistic work. There were times when Ruth and his girls could be with him, but to be on the road with three girls between three and seven years of age would be too high a price to pay for the rewards he envisioned in evangelism.

Then he received a call from an independent church in Lewiston, Idaho, looking for someone to temporarily fill the pulpit until a full-time minister could be found. He saw nothing negative about committing to that position. It would give his family some rest and would only require him to preach twice a week. After he had been there a few weeks, the board offered him the position as pastor.

There was a lot to like about the situation. There was plenty of room for growth with an auditorium that could seat 400-500. The church was located in downtown Lewiston, the heart of town. The board was enthusiastic about its new pastor and his family, pledging to support him in his relationships with OBC, their Bible college and camping programs.

A parsonage was furnished for the Stewarts, and they dug into their new pastorate with great enthusiasm. Youth for Christ had established a foothold in the community. Milton got acquainted immediately with Verle Bjur, the local director, a gifted young man recently graduated from Northwest College of Kirkland, Washington. Every Saturday night Milton was attending the meetings, playing his horn, leading in singing, or even speaking. His enthusiasm and love for the youth helped build the YFC program, and brought some new faces to his congregation. When asked to take a position on the local YFC board, he readily accepted.

As the strong and anointed biblical preaching flooded through Milton, people in his congregation began to be stirred. The most impressionable ones were teens from the Sunday school class he taught. When his young people got on fire for God, they wanted to make their lives count for eternity. What could they do? How could they prepare themselves for ministry?

Within the church outreach were street meetings to attend, tracts to pass out, witnessing groups to create, and the poor to clothe and feed. But for many, the answer was long range...they would enroll at Eugene Bible College, receive a thorough Bible education, and make themselves available for full-time Christian work.

As the months and years passed, Prayer League Tabernacle became the largest pipeline for new students among all the Open Bible churches in the Pacific Division. The college prized Lewiston's young people, as most of them were firmly grounded in the Word, and proved to be some of the most outstanding EBC scholars. One year alone, forty-seven left Lewiston for EBC in answer to God's call to prepare for ministry. Not only single people were leaving for Bible training, but a good number of young married couples dug up their Lewiston roots, transferring their whole families to Eugene for a complete change in their careers.

The first evangelists Milton invited to minister at Prayer League Tabernacle were the couple who had held fruitful healing meetings at his Martinez church.

They also ministered effectively in Lewiston, but one evening, without previous notice, Ruth was asked to testify about her healing in Martinez. She was a bit taken aback by being put on the spot because she still had physical symptoms of the breast lumps. What would she say? She determined to give God glory, so she simply stated she had been prayed for and, having sensed God's presence in her body, believed she was healed.

Later that week she lay awake in bed weeping over the predicament in which she found herself. She had told the congregation in Martinez, and now in Lewiston, that God had healed her. When discussing this earlier with Milton and her father, Mr. Phair had volunteered to pay for her surgery. That could have been done by the good Seventh Day Adventist physician in Martinez, but that opportunity was now history.

The heaviness was still on her heart the next day while she was vacuuming under her children's beds. She found herself saying, almost aloud, "I wish I hadn't told anybody that I was healed, and had just gone ahead and had the surgery!" Ruth and Milton lived in the Word of God and one of their promises was from Philippians 1:6 "...he who began a good work in you will carry it on to completion until the day of Christ Jesus." Ruth was convinced God had started a physical healing in her, but it was most difficult living on the human side of God's timing. In her heart of hearts, Ruth believed God was going to give her the victory, which would bring glory to Him. And having Milton beside her through this tough trial was great comfort.

The man preceding Milton at Prayer League Tabernacle was Pastor Cole. His wife's parents, Mr. and Mrs. Maston, lived in Lewiston, attending the church until the men of the board asked their son-in-law, Pastor Cole, to leave. Through this time of trial and disappointment, Mr. Maston was wounded in his spirit, vowing not to darken the door of the church again. There was no love lost between him and the church fathers.

Although Milton became aware of these matters, the Lord impressed on him to visit the Mastons and attempt to restore their standing. When he knocked at their door, Mrs. Maston greeted him warmly. After hearing Milton wanted to speak with her husband, she replied, "You know, it isn't going to do you a bit of good. He's out in the barn and you know he is angry about this whole mess. He won't come in to meet with you."

"Well," Milton replied, "I still want to talk with him, so I'll go out to the barn and speak with him there."

As Milton approached the barn, Mr. Maston, all six foot three of him, stood in the doorway watching him. He was wearing striped bib overalls, one strap buttoned, but the other side open and hanging off his shoulder.

After a brief, but somewhat pleasant exchange, Pastor Stewart asked, "How come you can't button that other side of your overalls?"

"I have this growth," Mr. Maston replied, opening his shirt and displaying a tumor the size of a grapefruit.

"God can heal that, you know," Milton said. Tears came to Mr. Mastons's eyes. Milton continued, "Do you mind if I pray for you right now?"

"No, that's fine," Mr. Maston said.

Pastor Stewart laid his hands on the man's shoulders, asking God to heal him. The presence of the Lord flooded the two men as they stood worshiping and thanking God for his goodness. After awhile, Mr. Maston checked himself again. The tumor was gone.

Two days later, Mr. Maston called the church office and asked Pastor Stewart, "If I come back to the church, do you think the people will receive me?"

Milton responded honestly, "I don't know if they will, but I can guarantee you that I will gladly welcome you anytime."

Sunday night after the service had started, the back door opened and in walked Mr. Maston. He made his way down the aisle into a pew near the front. Pastor Stewart introduced him to the congregation and invited him to the pulpit. In a humble and broken spirit, Mr. Maston apologized to the congregation for his attitude and bitterness of heart over the past events regarding his son-in-law. He asked them to forgive him, expressing his gratefulness for God's healing and mercy. God had not only healed his body, but reconciled a difficult, broken relationship.

A.C. Valdez Jr. Revival

When the idea came to hold a citywide revival meeting in Lewiston, A.C. Valdez Jr. came to Milton's mind. He had met his father early in his own ministry and led songs for him in a small Kansas town where Open Bible Churches' Gordon Peterson was pastoring. A.C. Valdez Sr. had come there to hold a tent revival. His son's ministry was notable. Tens of thousands of people packed his tent-revival meetings, especially in foreign countries. God confirmed His Word with signs and wonders through Valdez' ministry. Milton believed this was exactly what Lewiston needed in 1952.

It took several phone calls before Milton had Valdez on the line from Birmingham, England, where he was holding meetings. Valdez had a ten-day gap in his schedule about six months out, so could honor their request. As for the financial arrangements, A.C. Valdez Jr. made an unusual stipulation: "If you will take a love offering for me, I will be responsible for paying all the expenses of the meeting: my travel, your advertising and costs, rental of facilities...everything." What did they have to lose? Milton agreed, and they began to pray for a genuine visitation from God for Lewiston.

The church board got behind the meetings, and Milton began the organizational work of gathering a team of churches to help support the meetings and pray. Four pastors agreed to actively participate, and every night the revival was on, those four cancelled their own services and encouraged their people to come to Prayer League Tabernacle for the revival meetings. These pastors and church leaders were given responsibilities which included helping on the platform during services, organizing follow-up on the expected converts, and any other task the revival efforts needed accomplished. Full-page ads were placed in the Lewiston Tribune, which reached those 50 to 80 miles away, including many friends among the Nez Perce Indians.

The meetings were so successful, A.C. Valdez Jr. was invited to come back to Lewiston for a second series of revival meetings. What is reported here combines events from the two revivals of the early '50s.

The first couple of meetings found the church filled to less than capacity, but after several incredible miracles took place, the sanctuary began filling an hour before the service began. Parking was limited around the downtown building so a nearby Safeway store parking lot was used. The police were called following some Safeway complaints about customer space and congested streets. Several young Lewiston police officers volunteered their time each evening to direct traffic before the meetings started. Two of those men invited Christ into their lives during the revival.

The messages Valdez preached were very plain and direct. He was neither flamboyant nor especially polished in style, preaching simple sermons from the Word. "The greatest miracle God ever does," he said, "is to change the human heart." After preaching, he invited those wishing to receive Christ to come forward and present themselves at the altar. There were always respondents. Un-churched people came along with Catholics, Lutherans, and every imaginable denomination.

With the altar call completed, those who wanted prayer formed a line from the front altar space up the aisle to the back of the building. Cooperating ministers assisted the people, some of whom were on crutches or in wheel chairs. Others were standing with support from a friend or relative. They were brought up on the platform and prayed for in front of the audience. Valdez sometimes talked to them briefly or listened to their requests for prayer. He made it clear he had no power in himself to heal the sick. Only God could perform the miracle needed.

Milton and the steering committee knew the meetings needed a much larger facility for the Sunday evening services. The local college gymnasium with a two-thousand-seat capacity, plus floor space, was rented. Setting up an attractive platform at one end of the basketball court gave everybody a good seat. The building was packed, leaving standing room only.

For some, the revival meetings took on the air of a sideshow. Lewiston certainly had never seen anything like it before, and the happenings at Prayer League Tabernacle and in the college gym were the talk of the town. Though the seed of God's word was sown in all kinds of soils, the harvest from these revival meetings more than satisfied the expectations of the planners.

Documenting physical healing can sometimes be troublesome, but the following miracles and testimonies are offered here, authenticated by indisputable long-term results, immediately visible results, and a doctor's examination.

A young girl of about seven years of age was in the prayer line. She had special shoes designed to accommodate her clubfeet. Valdez prayed for her, then asked an assisting minister to remove the girl's shoes. The audience watched as her feet uncurled and straightened out to become normal. The girl's mother, sitting in the back of the church, realized what had happened. Running down the aisle weeping, she picked up her obviously healed daughter in her arms, making her way back to their seats.

About a year later Pastor Stewart was asked what eventually happened to the girl with the healed clubfeet. He told a sad story. The healing was genuine, but when he personally called on the family after the meetings, the mother's heart had somehow become hardened to the Lord. She ordered him off her porch and property. It is a mystery how someone could be so blessed by the miraculous power of Christ, then spurn God's servants who were instrumental in introducing them to this power and who continued to care for them.

Tony Muscat was an employee of Potlatch Forest, Inc. when he sustained a crippling injury. A beam fell on him, severing the Achilles tendon on his left foot. Tony was a faithful member of the Roman Catholic

Church in Lewiston. After attending one of Valdez' meetings, the next night he stood in the prayer line to see if God would heal him. After being prayed for, he felt a change in his foot. Walking outside the church, he sat down on the steps and took off his specially built shoe. He could hardly believe it! His Achilles tendon was completely healed. Tony was so full of joy he walked all over downtown Lewiston with one shoe on and the other off, telling everybody he met what God had done for him at the church at the bottom of 9th Street. Soon after his healing, Tony revisited the shoe store where he had been fitted with his special shoe. Seeing his healed foot, the store owner was dumbfounded. Tony proceeded to explain exactly what had happened to him through prayer. His testimony of God's power was told over and over throughout the city.

Carl Cromer, a big raw-boned former mill worker, attended the church. He and his wife were active in helping the young people's group and encouraging them to follow Christ. While Carl was working at Carpenter Lumber Company's mill south of town, a large piece of timber fell from a truck, crushing both legs. For seven years he had worn heavy metal braces from his thighs to his feet. During the meetings, Carl and his wife were at church every night. Finally, he began to believe God would heal him, so he joined the prayer line. Following prayer, he left the main sanctuary and headed back to the prayer room. Removing his braces, he happily marched out, demonstrating to the audience he could kneel, squat, walk and do anything a normal person could. He was totally healed. Since he continued to attend and work in our church, he was living evidence of God's healing power.

Joan (Davis) Lumbard was a high school graduate who had just been born again. Her activities in Youth for Christ brought her in touch with Verle Bjur, the YFC director, who had an Assembly of God background. He told her about God's ministry of healing, and she was invited to attend the Valdez meetings. Having been raised in a denominational church, she had never encountered anyone who believed God wanted to do miraculous things right now. After attending a meeting and witnessing the healing of the little girl's clubfeet, she became a believer. She entered the healing line to be prayed for the next Friday.

Joan suffered from an injury to her right knee in the ninth grade, tried various treatments, and then surgery after graduating from high school. A further injury to the knee left her with this diagnosis from a specialist: "I see no hope for flexibility in your knee, and you likely will suffer pain for the rest of your life." There were weekly cortisone injections under her kneecap. She could hardly bend her injured right knee. Even in driving, she used only her right foot on the accelerator because she needed the flexibility of her left foot for braking. (To this day, she still drives that way simply from her initial habit.)

Verle Bjur sat with her on the front row, along with friends from her musical group. That night the prayer line was long, but when she finally hobbled up the steps and stood before Brother Valdez, all he said was, "Do you believe God will heal you?" Replying with a genuine "Yes," she closed her eyes as the evangelist gently placed his hand on her forehead and prayed. She later described a sensation of heat saturating her knee, feeling like warm oil. She began walking across the stage toward the other steps where her friends were sitting. She thought about going down the steps her normal way, favoring her right knee, but she deliberately switched legs and stepped down. Joan would have fallen headlong had she not been healed! To the awestruck amazement of her front-row friends, she gracefully navigated the steps and sat down with them. Following the service, she went to the home of her friends, Van and Alice Jones, and repeatedly ran up and down their eleven porch steps.

Verle gave her Oral Roberts' book, *If You Need Healing Do These Things*, which she read from cover to cover. Going back to Dr. Douglas' office, she didn't tell him what had happened. As she lay on the examining table, he got out his measuring instrument to record the amount of flexibility in the knee. When he held her leg in the air and applied pressure, she relaxed her knee and it bent in a completely normal manner. He was absolutely startled. When Joan told him how God had healed her, he replied, "Joanie, doctors can only put things together. It is always God who heals." He was so happy for her!

For weeks after the meetings, reports came to the church of other miraculous healings. Sara Close, a young lady in our youth group, had been cross-eyed from an early age. After Valdez prayed for her she was completely healed and there was never any evidence of her former condition in the years her family attended the church. An eleven- year-old boy had broken his back and wore a heavy brace to stabilize his spine. After being prayed for, he went to the prayer room and removed the brace, leaving it at the church. A couple of weeks later he returned to pick up the brace as a remembrance of his healing. He went on to play football for Lewiston High School with never a trace of his former spinal problem.

The revival meetings were not without some opposition. Milton went to the Lewiston Tribune and spoke personally with the editor about the possibility of doing a feature story on the revival stirring the whole community. He was rebuffed by the editor with the words, "We don't run feature stories on such stuff as that!" The following day's feature story included a large picture of five elderly ladies with an accompanying article detailing their bridge party.

On the final Sunday evening meeting at the college gym, evangelist Valdez was incredibly burdened in his heart. As he gave the altar call, the Lord impressed on him that someone was getting a last chance to make his/her heart right before God. He spoke very directly to the audience, pleading with that individual to respond to God *tonight*. The invitation was prolonged perhaps 15 to 20 minutes as hundreds of people went forward to make sure their sins were forgiven and their hearts were in right standing with God. Following this unusual altar call, a few songs were sung while the healing line was formed. It was a sobering atmosphere, even through the joy of healing miracles that took place that night. The Lord made all acutely aware that decisions in this life, for or against Jesus Christ, will forever affect our eternal destiny. It seemed the presence of God, revealed in both His fear and in His incredible goodness, put the signature of God's blessing upon the entire revival.

Who can measure the results of such a revival meeting? The sheer numbers were astounding. Over one-fourth of the 10,000+ population of Lewiston had been in attendance at a single meeting. Nearly 700 cards were filled out in response to receiving Jesus Christ as personal Savior. It seemed nearly every family and business in the valley had been touched in some way by the revival meetings. There was a new openness in the town to talk about a personal God who had done the miraculous "right here in River City." Hundreds of people had been saved and healed by a gracious, loving Savior.

As promised, all the expenses for the revival meetings were fully paid by Valdez. For weeks after, the cooperating churches were bulging with those who had been touched by the living God. The pastors and congregations spent months following up those who received Christ as their personal Savior. It was a sovereign awakening from God, which had never been seen before in Lewiston, Idaho.

* * *

.

Chapter Six

Through a Teen's Eyes

"...how that from infancy you have known
the holy Scriptures which are able
to make you wise for salvation
through faith in Christ Jesus"
2 Timothy 3:15

I met him when I was thirteen. When he led singing
at our Youth for Christ rallies, his wholehearted
enthusiasm carried the day. His infectious personality bubbled over with the joy of the Lord. It was
no secret he was excited about his relationship with
Jesus Christ.

That summer of 1952, we held a citywide revival
in Lewiston, and the large evangelistic tent was set up
in a vacant lot on Main Street. A number of us kids
were there to unload old wooden pews and chairs for
our anticipated audience. While waiting for the next
truckload, we took the first pews, placed them ten

yards apart down the length of the tent, then began running hurdle races. That's when I got to know Milton Stewart. He was right there racing with us.

After we got a bit winded, we would lie on our backs, lock arms, and Indian wrestle. It was hard to believe I could have so much fun with an adult who wasn't even my pastor. He simply loved all of us kids and wanted us to know that having a great time wasn't a lost art when you were a Christian.

Our family had attended church from my earliest years. I was nine years old when I went forward, received Christ as my personal Savior, and was baptized. Our church changed pastors, and the new minister devoted the bulk of his sermon time to current events. We didn't hear much about a personal relationship with Jesus Christ.

Through family friends, we became aware of the Youth for Christ Bible Club meetings at a church near our public school. It was there I met a group of young people who were excited about loving and following Jesus Christ. My heart was touched, and God's love began to awaken my spirit through connections with these new friends.

Tragedy struck our home right after the Christmas holidays; my father was hospitalized after having collapsed from hemorrhaging. He was diagnosed with stomach ulcers and underwent a successful operation. Following a dose of incorrect medication, he developed hepatitis and, after a six-week battle, passed away. The loss left our family numb and seemingly directionless without our godly father.

My mother, Irma Bennett, sought the Lord daily for strength. She believed God was able to be her husband and her children's father.

One of the biggest issues we faced was the question of where we would attend church. Through our exposure to Youth for Christ, Lynn, my older sister, and I knew other young people were getting fed spiritually in several churches. Lynn's best high school friends attended the Baptist church. My Youth For Christ buddy, Chuck Jones, had started attending Prayer League Tabernacle where Brother Stewart was pastor, so I opted to join him there. On Sunday mornings, Mom let me off at the top of the hill near Prayer League Tabernacle, drove by the Baptist church to deposit Lynn, then proceeded to the Nazarene Church where she and Eve worshipped. We had some interesting conversations around the dinner table on Sunday afternoons.

Brother Stewart marvelously balanced preaching the Word of God and allowing the Holy Spirit to work among the people. There was an expectation the Spirit would make God's Word come alive to us, and I recall being so excited I would get goose bumps on my arms. I even said to my friends, in ignorance, "See these goose bumps? They always appear when the Holy Ghost is on me!"

One evening before the evangelistic service began, a group of young people were praying in the basement of the church. When I went down to join them, I saw the teenagers were praying all over the room, some on their knees, some lying prostrate on the floor, others standing quietly in worship. Nobody was out of control, but some young people were speaking in other tongues in their worship of God. Since this was all new to me, I decided my mother ought to see what was taking place here, so I called her. When she arrived, I introduced her to Brother Stewart, and she earnestly watched the students in prayer. She did not say a lot about what she observed, but she did feel the sincerity of the young people and their heart-felt prayers.

Many teenagers, encouraged by our pastor, were baptized in the Holy Spirit, and I observed this phenomenon with great interest. Our ranks swelled during the summer with the return of students from Eugene Bible College. Their maturity in the Lord was winsome and the genuineness of their faith made me hunger all the more for this baptism in the Holy Spirit.

At that time it was the custom of Pentecostal churches to have "tarrying meetings" where people waited for the Holy Spirit to come upon them, much like the apostles waited in the upper room in Acts 1 and 2. On a Sunday evening after I had turned four-teen, I had had enough of this tarrying and made up my mind that if the Lord wanted me to receive the Holy Spirit, tonight would be the night. Speaking in tongues was a bit of a roadblock for me. It took awhile to realize the Holy Spirit wasn't going to take my tongue and begin to speak for me. I was worried that if I began saying unintelligible things, even though I very much sensed God's presence upon me, it would be my flesh speaking. A friend helped me through that barrier and I finally let go and began worshiping God in a new and creative way. It was a baptism into the love and presence of Jesus. Wow! What holiness! What sacred presence! What longing for more of Him!

When Pastor Stewart asked me about my experience, he didn't ask if I had received the baptism in the Holy Spirit; he asked if I was satisfied I had received what God had promised. I thought about the question quite a while before answering him. Recalling a phrase I had heard him say, I replied, "I am satisfied, but with an unsatisfied satisfaction." Being introduced to the life of the Spirit only left me desiring more.

Because I didn't have a dad and hungered for things of the Lord, Brother Stewart took a special interest in me. He would look me in the eye and tell me he loved me and prayed for me. He told me God had His hand on my life, and as I walked with Him He would use me for His glory. These verbal affirmations began to create passion and real growth in my Christian life.

While listening to Brother Stewart preach one day, I made a quirky decision to be able to locate every verse he referred to from the pulpit. If I heard the verse or story a second time, I wanted to know where it was by book, chapter, and verse. This put me seriously in the Word every Sunday afternoon. I began memorizing verses, then sections of Scripture. The more I was in the Word, the more alive and real Christ became to me. I was introduced to the Navigator's Topical Memory System and also memorized 'chunks' of Scripture God had impressed upon my heart. God's Word became a personal love letter to me from Jesus.

Since I had been playing keyboard for years, I was asked to help out on the piano during church services and, later on in high school, the concert grand Hammond organ became available to me. But the most fun I had in my keyboard work was accompanying Brother Stewart's cornet playing. I was certainly not in the same technical league as he, but he put up with me. We had fun playing some neat arrangements for Youth for Christ, including "Onward Christian Soldiers" and "The Trumpeter's Holiday."

During the winter of my junior year of high school, I would come down to the church after school and practice on the church's organ. On more than one occasion I entered the empty and darkened church only to hear Brother Stewart praying back in the prayer room. He prayed like he lived, wholeheartedly and out loud. One day I stood silently alone in the center of the sanctuary listening to him praying for me. I felt like removing my shoes as Moses did before the Lord in the desert. His prayers touched me deeply.

The Stewarts had a weekly radio program they recorded from the altar area of the main sanctuary. On occasion I would accompany a special number or play background music from the organ. With the microphones and recorder in place, a large clock with a red warning light was prominently placed in front of the microphones. Brother Stewart would introduce himself, the origin of the program, the special music, and then preach. It was like there was an audience of thousands in front of him. His messages were solid Gospel and spoken with great conviction. He always had difficulty winding down and not going over his time allotment. Much to the credit of the radio station, their engineers often stretched out his "overtime" a bit so his message could be concluded. We would sometimes tease him, "Why use a clock? You never look at it anyway!" He took our ribbing with good humor.

A significant number of Nez Perce Indians from Kamiah heard the radio messages and gave their hearts to Christ. Among them was a lady we knew as Sister Sunshine and her daughter Wapshili. Along with a number of their friends, they often journeyed to Lewiston for evening services or special revival meetings. When we found the Indian friends had no place of worship, the men of the church went to Kamiah and built a small sanctuary for their gatherings. The love and warmth of those people toward the Stewarts was incredible. They felt the Stewarts were as much Nez Perce as any of their own people. Every year at Ruth's birthday, Wapshili would make her a beautiful beaded purse. When they were sick, they might show up at Stewarts' door, asking for their prayers. Years later in their ministry, they met Wapshili at Faith Temple in Tacoma. Wapshili reminded them of the day she came to their door with a badly swollen, infected ankle from getting tangled in barbed wire. When the Stewarts prayed for her, God graciously healed her.

As much as any man I have known, Brother Stewart lived in the life of the Holy Spirit on a daily basis. A core belief of his was that God was the same now as He was in biblical times, and we needed to expect the same results through our faith in Him and His Word. Through the weekly ministry of the church, we heard God's Word faithfully proclaimed, saw the gifts of the Holy Spirit in operation, witnessed miracles, heard testimonies of God's healings, and rejoiced when new believers were added to our fellowship.

The entire Stewart family elevated the church's attractiveness to the Lewiston community. On Sunday mornings the three Stewart girls often sang a beautifully arranged trio, accompanied by their mother. Pam, Pat, and Bobbi Jo would be spotless in their freshly ironed clothes, cute hairdos, and glowing faces. They sang in three-part harmony, even though the youngest girls were barely school age. Ruth played the violin at a professional level. Milton's rich cornet melodies filled the sanctuary. The duets sung by Ruth and Milton touched our hearts deeply. In addition to hearing the solid gospel message, it was a first-class presentation at Prayer League Tabernacle.

About the time my sister Lynn left home for college in South Carolina, Mom was invited by a family friend to attend a local revival meeting at an Assembly of God church. The evangelist was passionate about helping people receive the baptism in the Holy Spirit. Mom had visited my church several times and witnessed the moving of the Spirit, so there was hunger in her heart for more of God. After

Mother was filled with the Holy Spirit, she went back to her pastor and shared with him this precious experience. He was considerably less than enthusiastic about her testimony. Mother strongly felt she needed encouragement in the Spirit-filled life, and shortly thereafter she and Eve began attending our church.

During my first years at Prayer League Tabernacle, I was not aware of the unusual way our independent church was organized. Four men had purchased the building, and those men served as the un-elected board of the church. They not only owned the building, but also were responsible for the personnel, finances, and future direction of this independent assembly. For reasons I did not understand, some men of the board became very hostile toward Pastor Stewart. Finally, a meeting was called one Sunday evening for all who were interested in the future of their church. Brother Stewart opened the meeting, then invited the board to address the congregation. No reasons were given, but the board announced they had decided not to retain Milton Stewart as pastor. He was officially removed from his duties at Prayer League Tabernacle.

Over the next week or two, more than half the congregation made unsolicited calls to the Stewarts, declaring their loyalty to them. Milton felt God had not unburdened his heart for the Lewiston area, so he called his denominational leaders and received permission to start a new Open Bible church in the valley. Our first meeting place was a VFW building in Clarkston, Washington, our twin city across the

Snake River. We had to clean and fumigate the place after Saturday night dances to make it habitable for church on Sunday mornings.

Months later we had the opportunity to purchase the historical Idaho Law Library building in a park, strategically located above the shopping area of downtown Lewiston. This was one of Idaho's earliest government buildings. We set aside a time for people to bring a special offering to secure a down payment for this future church home. Less than twenty people were in attendance at that meeting, but it became a significant milepost in my early Christian life.

As I prayed about this offering, I knew I would be lucky to come up with $100 for a gift out of my after-school job at Pepsi Cola Bottlers. Then I remembered Mom and Dad had set aside some savings bonds for my college education. These amounted to a couple thousand dollars, and represented everything my folks had saved for my education. I went to Mother and asked her if we could donate that money to the church for the down payment. Even as a write this, I tremble to think my mother would even consider doing such a thing, but she did. We gave the whole amount.

Out of that group of people came cash, money from the sale of land in Arizona, promissory notes, wedding rings, and other valuables given in faith and love to the work of the Lord. Unbelievable sacrifices were made by people who had very little. The amount received was more than enough to secure the down payment, and we began the tough work of changing a stone edifice of law into a house of grace.

After giving away my savings, how was it possible I spent over seven years in college and graduate school with minimal debt? God providentially supplied my educational needs. I received two separate and unsolicited scholarships totaling more than twice the amount of money we had given to the church. I became a Christian school principal, and the school board of directors paid for all of my graduate studies. Through the years I have seldom questioned how I could afford to tithe and give. God has proven Himself over and over again as the Source of our supply. You can't out-give Him. As for my mother, she was beyond frugal. She sacrificed for all of us, worked until she was eighty, helped all her children purchase their first homes, and gave abundantly to the Lord's kingdom. She certainly will have plenty of treasure in heaven!

The removal of the wall between the two government chambers was the largest and most critical part of the renovation of this law library. Van R. Jones, my buddy's dad, used his crane to insert a large I-Beam across the rooms to support the roof. Almost single handedly, he financed the renovation of that building, using his heavy equipment and building experience. When we tore down that huge wall with sledgehammers, picks and shovels, the plaster, bricks and stones flew everywhere. Brother Stewart was in the middle of this whole scene of carnage, having more fun than anybody. The dust was choking, and when we emerged from the building we looked like "whitened sepulchers."

At a Saturday work party, Max Harris, one of the church's teenagers, brought his family's pickup to help haul junk to the dump. We had attempted to give away the hundreds of leather-bound law books stored throughout the building, but without success. My sister Eve, Pam Stewart, and a friend, Kareen Olson, helped Max load his pickup, then crawled in the back on top of the books for the trip to the dump. The sixth-grade girls were given a good lecture on safety and the importance of staying seated while the pickup was in motion. On the way up the hill to the dump, Eve stood up briefly to see over the top of the cab. At that moment, the pickup hit a pothole in the road and swerved. Eve fell backwards, her momentum carrying her over the tailgate, which she caught with her legs. Her hands scraped the pavement below, but her two friends grabbed her legs and somehow pulled her back into the loaded pickup. The panic-stricken girls cuddled together for the remainder of the trip. Max was unaware of the happenings in the back of his truck, so they were sure their misadventure would remain a personal secret.

They returned to the church where they were met by their pastor. Milton had a worried look on his face as he asked the group, "Are you kids okay?" The girls nodded. Again he asked, "Are you sure you're alright?" Getting a second group of nods, he said, "A short time after you left here, God placed an incredible burden on my heart for you. I went into the prayer room and interceded for you kids. I don't know what it's all about, but I'm glad you are okay." The girls never told their pastor what had happened that day in the back of Max's pickup. I only became aware of it in the writing of this biography.

During the summer prior to my senior year in high school, God spoke to my heart about his will for my life. I hadn't had any clarity about what vocation God wished me to pursue. Some felt I could be used of God in music because I had exercised some gifts and served the church in a small way. I loved athletics and received inquiries about whether I would want to play football at the college level. All those questions were settled one day while lying on my bed on the back porch of our home. The Lord spoke to my heart in a soft, but clear way, "I want you to preach the Gospel of Jesus Christ."

I readied myself to go to Eugene Bible College and see what the Lord had in store for me through preparation there. It was hard to leave Lewiston and especially difficult to leave the Stewart family. My sister had become best friends with Stewart's oldest daughter Pam, and our two families adopted one another as much more than friends. I not only respected Brother Stewart, I loved and admired him like a dad.

The summer prior to Bible college, Milton was invited to be the camp speaker at the Northern California Open Bible Church Youth Camp out of Santa Cruz, California. He invited my Christian buddy, Paul Bailey, and me to go along with him. We were camp counselors, which helped pay for our expenses. Leaving Lewiston after work on an August evening, we found ourselves motoring through the eastern Oregon desert in the middle of the night. We were jolted out of our midnight mental fog by on-the-spot radio coverage of an invasion of the eastern United States by aliens from outer space. We were shocked and dumbfounded for a few minutes in that speeding car, until we realized this was a rebroadcast of the infamous Orson Welles's "War of the Worlds" from 1938. How we laughed and kidded each other about that one!

We arrived in Port Chicago, California, on Saturday afternoon. Milton preached in Herb Bradshaw's Open Bible Church Sunday morning, but neither of us fellows could remember what he preached. I guess we were a bit distracted by Bradshaw's attractive teenage daughter. She told us she would be happy to show us around camp, and we were more than happy to be shown. Some of the extras we enjoyed on this trip included a visit to Golden Gate Park in San Francisco, a tour of the Winchester Mystery House, and an exciting first-time ride on a roller coaster at Santa Cruz. Milton had as much fun as we did on that ride. Being around him in a relaxed atmosphere reminded me of the great fun we had playing cards or table games at their home. Ruth really loved games, and they were exactly that to her—games! The rules weren't as important as having fun, and as the games went along, Ruth was responsible for some very unpredictable things that happened. Let me say it this way, she very appropriately lived up to the nickname we attached to her—"Sister Cheat!" But back to the camp meeting.

Observing the influence of my pastor on these young campers was enlightening. Since I had always worked through the summer months, I had never been to an Open Bible Church Youth Camp. The entire camp, especially the evening evangelistic meetings, was focused on the spiritual revitalization of the young people. Brother Stewart's sermons were alive and relevant. One evening he preached a sermon entitled "A Tale of Two Men, and the Love of One Sin." This was the story of John the Baptist, King Herod, Salome, and her mother, Herodias. There were always times of prayer following the preaching, and Brother Stewart mingled among the students, praying for and encouraging them. Early in the morning he woke the camp with a rousing reveille on his cornet; late that night closed the day playing "Taps." He had a great way of affirming these young campers and encouraging them in their dedication to Christ.

It is impossible to weigh the influence of one man, Milton Stewart, on my life. I learned in a personal and practical way, through his preaching and his life, that what God says about us in His Word is true. Christ emptied Himself of everything, took our sins upon Him on the cross, and died a horrible death so He could reconcile us to Himself and have communion with us again. When Christ reigns in our lives and the Holy Spirit fills our being, we exude His nature to those about us. We are special, not in a puffed-up way, but each of His children has the eternal mark of the Divine One upon his being.

Milton loves the Word of God, which he has faithfully preached since he was saved. One of our adult church members commented that Brother Stewart could have had the biggest congregation in town if he had determined to do it. He had unlimited enthusiasm, a great way of working with people, and plenty of leadership ability. But he was resolved to preach the Word in faithfulness to God, not to strive for great numbers, nor to be caught up in church fads. He remained a biblical purist and an uncompromising soldier of the cross.

Prior to leaving for Eugene Bible College, I asked Brother Stewart if he would write a note of encouragement in my Bible. I'll close with his words from inside the front cover.

To my Son in the faith of our Lord Jesus Christ

Dear John,

May the grace of God keep you
Weak enough to always lean on His strength
Foolish enough to always depend on His wisdom
Humble enough to always give Him the glory
Broken enough to always be heard at His throne
Poor enough to always be seeking His riches

Thou therefore, my son, be strong in the grace that is in Christ Jesus.
Thou therefore endure hardness as a good soldier of Jesus Christ.

It is impossible to put into words what is in my heart concerning you. Please Him, (our loving and gracious Saviour) and I shall be happy and grateful beyond measure.

My mother gave me a little proverb as a young man. I'll close with it:
'My strength is as the strength of ten because my heart is pure.'

God's richest and fullest blessing is my constant prayer for you. I'm proud of you.

Your pastor, friend, brother in Christ, but more.

In His love,

Pastor M. J. Stewart

* * *

Chapter Seven

Tough Times for Tough People

"I can do everything through him who gives me strength." Philippians 4:13

The Stewarts had always faced the future with great optimism and an expectancy of God's blessing. Starting this new Open Bible Church in Lewiston, however, would pose problems that would test them to the core. Ruth still was bothered with lumps in her breasts; the financial condition of this church was less stable than that of their former one; the converted law library building was a challenge in both design and maintenance. Overarching these difficulties was the brooding sense that Milton's character had been denigrated by his dismissal from Prayer League Tabernacle.

But the Stewarts were not alone. They were pastors to people who loved them and believed God had called them to continue to nourish their congregation in the Word and the Spirit-filled life. The connection between pastors and this group of Open Bible Church worshipers was forged in love and trust. It was an unusual bond with multiple dimensions. It was true not many moneyed families were among this band, and a host of young leaders were being educated at Eugene Bible College, but those forming the church body were faithful, loyal, and generous.

Housing for the Stewart family came in miraculous fashion through Conrad and Lillian Priess. This couple offered to sell the Stewarts their rental house with no money down, a monthly payment, and the liberty to change their payment amount according to their ability to pay. The house was seven blocks from the church, had two main-level bedrooms, and two additional bedrooms in the basement. With housing taken care of through this blessing, the Stewarts went on to sign papers for, and enjoy the comforts of, a newer yellow station wagon.

After the church had operated a few months, however, the realities of the budget began to hit. There were the usual monthly bills for the mortgage, fuel, utilities, and salaries, with precious little left for the larger issues of maintenance and physical improvements on an old building. The former law library was heated with its original, antiquated large furnace, the lights were inadequate, the entire interior needed a facelift, and Sunday school rooms had to be built and furnished. The old law books nobody wanted were used to heat the church that first year. Still, it was most difficult to make ends meet, and the

Stewarts suffered the embarrassment of having their lovely station wagon repossessed.

Milton's heart had been broken by the schism in the Prayer League Tabernacle church. He loved every person in that congregation and had faithfully preached the whole Gospel of Christ to them. Lewiston was not a large town, and whenever he met one of his former congregants, he felt the pain of their separation. It was not a shallow hurt; it felt like an open wound. While walking down 5th Street toward Anderson's Department Store one day, Milton suddenly felt like he was physically paralyzed. He stood immobilized for a few minutes, then from his heart cried out, "Lord, don't you feel I've been humiliated enough?"

From this pit of despair, the Lord spoke into his heart a message of hope he would carry the rest of his life. He turned around and slowly limped back up the hill to the church. There he prostrated himself before God in prayer. "Lord, is the anointing You have given me for ministry gone? Will we ever see Your hand of blessing and visitation again?"

God's answer was larger than his questions. "There will be another visitation of the Holy Spirit." In his heart Milton asked when that might be. The response the Lord spoke was, "John the Baptist came as a forerunner to Christ. In the same way, a mighty visitation of my Holy Spirit will precede my coming in glory." Milton's heart and spirit were lifted by these words of the Lord, as well as Psalm 118:23, which was impressed upon his heart, "This is the Lord's doing, and it is marvelous in our eyes."

When God chooses to move, nothing can stand in His way. Milton knew he must continue to walk moment by moment in the presence of the Holy Spirit and encourage his congregation to experience the glorious moving of the Holy Spirit. His passion to live in the presence of God was not a selfish ambition, but his heart yearned to see the entire church of Jesus Christ walking in the power of the Spirit. His biblical teaching on the subject became a central theme in his ministry.

In summary, he taught that the church is to be energized by the Holy Spirit. God gives a great variety of gifts to individuals for the building up of the church, which 1 Corinthians 12-14 explains. There are also varieties of ministries within the church, explained in Ephesians 4:11-12. Romans 12 shows further gifts that are more motivational. Although it is important to recognize our gifts and the gifts of others in the body of Christ, the most important element Milton preached was simply walking in the Spirit with the fruit of the Holy Spirit evident in the life of the maturing believer. This was not a walk founded upon emotional ecstasy, but a walk of faith in the truths of God's Word. He saw, from the teachings of Paul and the examples of Christ and the apostles, it was not only possible to walk in the Spirit, but this was the norm God desired for all believers.

Milton's Sunday sermon subject one Sunday was the body of Christ caring for one another. He told of sitting on the basement steps of his home the night before, shining his daughters' shoes. It was getting late. He had to preach the next morning. Why in the world would he be shining these shoes at this time of the night? Two words came to his mind — "just because:" just because I love them, just because they are precious to me, just because it needs to be done, just because I want to. The message went to the heart of his listeners and "just-because" notes and deeds of kindness began showing up, many directed toward their beloved pastors.

The Stewarts wanted to see the hearts of God's people ignited by the Spirit of God, for without that, the church was simply going through the motions. In response to the urge of the Spirit, one weekend Milton and Ruth set aside those two days to fast and pray for revival in their church. Humbling themselves in gunnysack clothing, they spent all day Saturday and through the night in prayer and fasting at the church. Returning home early Sunday, they dressed for church and went back to lead the morning service.

There are innumerable Sundays in the span of a pastor's term, all having distinct presentations and results. Probably many could be documented and recorded, but most are not. This particular Sunday began like any other worship day; the family was dressed in their Sunday best, notes were looked at for the last time, there was a sweet presence of the Lord as they worshiped together and shared the Word. Altogether, a great time in God's house. Today, however, God had something very special for the Stewarts. As the service was coming to an end, Earl

Johnson made an announcement, "After the service has been dismissed, we would like the congregation to gather on the front lawn."

But we're getting ahead of ourselves. Before that time, the Johnsons, who owned an auto repair shop, had been looking for an opportunity to fix up a car for their family. A Buick that had been in an accident was brought in, and while fixing it, Earl decided it would make the perfect family car. He finished it off with a beautiful black enamel paint job. It was then the Lord spoke distinctly to Earl, "I want you to give this car to the Stewarts." His wife, Fern, was asleep when he shook her gently saying, "The Lord wants us to give the car to the Stewarts." There was no movement from Fern. Again, he shook his wife and said, "Fern, I believe the Lord wants us to give that Buick to the Stewarts." Fern opened an eye and replied, "Well, go ahead and give it to them, but let me go back to sleep."

Now, back to Sunday's gathering on the lawn. When the congregation walked out of the building, parked on the lawn was this lovely car with a large ribbon around it. There was a great celebration with tears of joy over this magnanimous just-because gift. Earl and Fern Johnson continued to serve the Lord faithfully. They were called to the ministry and became beloved pastors of several Open Bible churches, mainly in the Midwest.

Then, there was the widow with teenagers of her own who had a special burden for the Stewart children. These girls were getting into junior and senior high school, and there wasn't enough money to purchase new school clothes for them. Joined by two other ladies in the church, she collected yardage ends from the local JC Penney store, watched sales at the Hollywood Shoppe, and sewed outfits for the girls. These clothing gifts continued through Stewarts' ministry in Lewiston. The ladies even saw that each girl had a coveted new Jantzen sweater at the beginning of every school year, and it was all just-because. The message of "just-because" was felt by those prompted to act on it, as well as those who were recipients of it—God blessed the soul-felt message His obedient servant delivered.

Each summer Milton continued to preach at church youth camps. If the camp were close enough, the whole family went. It was not what some would consider a vacation, but for one week each year, that is how their vacation time was spent; it was one of the Stewarts; "just-because" gifts to their Lord. Through his ministry, Milton visited every OBC District Youth Camp in America. He not only was thrilled about ministering to teenagers, but he was able to build relationships with other church pastors and youth leaders.

In these early years of ministry, he longed for the interaction of older experienced men who would mentor him. In some instances he felt he was "working without a net" as much of his advice and examples came from his own experiences. As he matured and grew, he saw himself becoming that man to others as he developed a passion to mentor and encourage his young fellow pastors. Birthed in his spirit was the prayer, "God, make me a pastor of these men."

When God wants to do something special, it is often surprising how He works. At the Bible college in Eugene, Oregon, two married men from Lewiston, Ralph Stueber and Elmer White, were going through a period of fasting and prayer. They were impressed by the Lord to end this special time in Lewiston, so they drove home and spent a of couple days with their pastors. These men loved the Stewarts and had a great time of fellowship with them. As they were preparing to leave, the Stewarts gathered with them in the living room for a time of prayer.

Elmer turned to Ruth and asked, "Sister Stewart, have you ever testified about something God did for you about which you wish you had never spoken?"

Ruth was taken aback by the question. She thought the only ones knowing about her ongoing breast problems were her husband and her father. She turned to Milton and asked, "Why did you tell them about this?"

"I didn't say a thing to them, Ruth." There was an awkward pause, then Milton said, "Honey, this is not from men; this is from God. Let's praise Him for the answer." Lifting their hands together, the group began worshiping the Lord. God's presence descended and they basked in His goodness. After the men left, Ruth found all evidence of the breast problems had disappeared. It had been over five years since this condition first became apparent in Martinez. Although she trusted God's ability to heal her, the presence of those sore lumps were physical reminders of her mortality. It was hard to shake the foreboding that they would lead to an early death.

That God would use such a humble man as Elmer White to deliver this word of knowledge to Ruth amazed the Stewarts. Elmer was a very young Christian, and the Stewarts had never known him to exercise any gift of the Holy Spirit. It was from his mouth, however, that words came leading to Ruth's miracle deliverance from this awful condition. There was great rejoicing within the Stewart household as they embraced God's miraculous healing.

Irma Bennett, the author's mother, attended a women's meeting at the church when Ruth shared her testimony. She told her daughter Eve the following details: Ruth told the women of the Martinez doctor's exam, the prayers of the evangelist, her testimonies of healing, her father's offer to pay for surgery, her doubts and struggles with continuing symptoms, and God's healing touch of her body. For the occasion, Ruth was dressed in a lovely peplum-sculpted suit. Referring to her past wearing of this outfit, she said, "I could hardly get this on because it was so tight in the bust. Now look at all the room I have!"

Although there had been no conclusive diagnosis of Ruth's condition, the symptoms were real and certainly would have frightened any woman. Ruth doggedly hung on to the promises of God, trusting her life to His care. This took place over fifty years ago, and Ruth has been symptom-free since then. The Stewarts believe strongly in praying for the sick, but they have never encouraged any to avoid consulting their doctors in times of illness.

Several weeks following Ruth's healing, she began to have a repetitive dream. On three separate nights she thought she heard the Lord saying to her, "I am going to bless your home with a son!" After the third dream, she told Milton her imagination was running wild. "Can you believe this crazy dream I'm having?" she said. Telling Milton her dream, he replied, "I believe that is the Lord." And it was, for within a year, their family was blessed by the arrival of John Milton Stewart.

The following examples are cited to give further accounts of God's healings during the ministry of Milton and Ruth in Lewiston.

Milton purchased a pair of cowboy boots for his son John from the owner of a shoe store on Main Street. A couple of weeks later he brought in a pair of shoes to be repaired and found this man sitting behind the counter with one foot wrapped and elevated. After exchanging some pleasantries and finding out how tough the owner was feeling, Pastor Stewart said, "We believe God answers prayer. Would you like me to pray for you?"

Thinking Milton would go back to the church to have the congregation pray, the owner said, "Sure, that would be fine." To his surprise, Milton walked around the counter, and laying his hands on the man's leg, prayed for his healing.

A week or so later, Milton was in the store to pick up his shoes. Spotting Milton, the owner grinned, saying, "You know, Reverend, it's really amazing. My foot was so blinkety-blankety bad...now look at this." With that, he began stamping his foot on the floor, grinning from ear to ear.

In a few months, this store owner made a decision to run for mayor of Lewiston. It was known that the incumbent mayor and the local fire chief owned and operated a house of prostitution east of town. When Milton visited the shoe store again, the owner asked him for his vote. Thinking about it, Milton decided he had a once-in-a-lifetime deal going here. His bargaining power? His vote. "If you are elected mayor and promise to dismiss the fire chief, I will not only vote for you," Milton said, "I will encourage my congregation to also support you." The storeowner and Milton shook on the deal. After being elected mayor, he was as good as his word, dismissing the fire chief and closing the house of prostitution.

An elderly woman in the church, Mrs. Daggett, came to the evening service one Sunday in great pain. She asked for prayer, and as the congregation gathered around her, it was obvious she was bloated and suffering intensely. At home that night, she passed a number of tumors, filling a four-quart kettle. Her husband, who was hostile to the things of the Lord, scoffed and insisted she take her tumors to the hospital and get a check up. The following morning, she obliged and had her doctor give her a thorough exam. What remained of the tumors in her body was a tiny spot smaller than a little fingernail. The doctor identified it as the place where the other tumors had been attached. He was flabbergasted, declaring, "Mrs. Daggett, you have been healed!"

During the later years of their ten-year ministry in Lewiston, Milton and Ruth took a break from their pastoral duties and served as evangelists for OBC. They rented a home in Springfield, Oregon, so they could be near Ruth's parents and the kids could attend a neighborhood school. While Milton was holding meetings for his friend, Herb Bradshaw, at the Port Chicago Open Bible Church, he developed a urinary problem. This was unknown to Ruth and the family, but the Lord laid a burden on their hearts to pray for their dad. When they finished their prayer time, Ruth suggested they take out a handkerchief, lay hands on it in prayer, and send it to their father. Everyone placed hands on the hankie, prayed for dad, tucked the cloth and a note into an envelope, and sent it off. Similar acts of faith are recorded in Acts 19.

Sunday evening, Milton was in such pain he almost cancelled his scheduled revival meeting. Whether right or wrong, he had an aversion to visiting a doctor's office. He considered Jesus his Great Physician, and would, as first course, call on Him for both his physical and spiritual needs. With great effort, he finished his sermon, prayed for many around the altar then started back to the parsonage, which was within walking distance. He was in such discomfort he was forced to crawl a good measure of the way.

The following morning, he wrote a note to his family asking them to anoint a hankie and send it to him. When he arrived at the post office to mail his letter, the envelope from his family was there to greet him. Taking the handkerchief back to his room, he laid it on his body and worshiped the Lord. God gave him immediate relief and thoroughly healed his urinary infection, accounting for another healing miracle—his own.

God often expanded Milton's ministry through the gifts of prophecy; God is communicating with his children today, and as we are open to the voice of the Holy Spirit, He will speak through us. Sometimes it will be a word of knowledge, at other times it will be a word of counsel or wisdom for a certain situation. As God worked through the gift of prophecy, Milton learned to listen clearly to God's message and then, with wisdom and love, speak the Lord's word as He directed. Many have been blessed and encouraged through this prophetic gift.

Conrad and Lillian Priess were enjoying their retirement. At an evening service, many were gathering around the altar for prayer. A number were ill and had come forward to be healed. As prayer was going on at the altar, Mr. Priess got out of his seat and started to come forward. Milton caught his attention saying, "Conrad, you don't need to come down here for prayer. God has already healed you!" For days, Conrad had been in pain with a double hernia. Immediately he began patting his body to see if the bulges and pain were still present. Finding nothing at all, he sat down and thanked the Lord for his healing. As he and his wife drove home that night, he found two sacks of feed had been left at the entrance to his driveway. Stopping the car, he picked up the feed sacks and carried them to the barn. Lillian wasn't too happy with him for testing the Lord in that way, but Conrad suffered no pain and returned immediately to a normal level of activity.

In the following story, I am using fictitious names. Milton did not often go to attorneys' offices, but this day he was on a mission. Entering the office, he introduced himself and asked the receptionist if he could see attorney Peterson; his business would only take a few minutes. The receptionist went to an office door, tapped lightly, opened the door and spoke quietly for a brief time. Turning to Milton, she said, "Mr. Peterson will see you now," and held the door open for their guest.

The two men exchanged greetings, then Milton backed away a step and said, "Mr. Peterson, it has come to my attention that you have been seeing Patty Lawrence, one of my church members. You have no real personal interest in her except to swindle her recent inheritance from her. I am here to tell you to leave her alone. Do you understand?" Mr. Peterson stammered a bit, then became angry. "Get out of my office you two-bit preacher!" he yelled. Milton went to the door, turned around and faced Mr. Peterson again and firmly said, "I'm going, but you make sure you leave Patty alone." With that, he turned on his heel and left.

What had precipitated this face-to-face encounter? The previous day, Patty had come to the church office to talk with her pastor. She told him Mr. Peterson had recently begun seeing her. Flowers, candy and other romantic gifts accompanied this sudden interest. Although she was flattered to be so sought after, a mental red flag told her something was a bit askew.

It didn't take Milton long to fill in the dots. Mrs. Lawrence had inherited a significant piece of property, and Mr. Peterson could see the opportunity of quick financial gain by befriending the recipient. Since there were legal papers needing to be handled through an attorney's office, Milton was more than willing to head off an attempt to swindle one of his flock. The visit was effective, and Mr. Peterson was history in Patty's life.

The church's location on the corner of the park was far enough from family residences to cause very few complaints. One evening, however, the police arrived at the church with a complaint from a neighbor about too much noise coming from the upper east room. The teenagers had gathered to pray and, on a hot summer day with the windows open, their prayers could be heard from some distance. The two summoned police officers went outside to sense the effect. What they found were young folk, not drinking or participating in a wild party, but having their time of prayer. When they reported back to Milton, they commended the youth and added that the neighbors had a problem if they couldn't put up with a little prayer.

When the Millers came to hold revival meetings, God did some powerful things. Jesse Ortiz was a handyman/roofer who had a big redheaded man working for him. This man was not a Christian, but agreed to come to the meetings with Jesse. God got a hold of his heart; he received Christ as his personal Savior, then was filled with the Holy Spirit. A short time after this drastic change in his life, his wife left him. He was greatly disappointed, but he knew Christ had made him a new creature and he continued to grow in his faith. The church's youth were especially moved during this revival, dedicating their lives to Christ and opening their hearts to God's call to ministry.

One of the young women who was a vital part of the congregation was Surena Harding. She had come to Lewiston from Orofino to attend business school and was employed at a local bank. Surena found her church home at Lewiston's Open Bible Church, providing leadership among the young people. After two years, she moved out of the area but kept in touch with the Stewarts. The following is a letter Milton wrote in reply on March 31, 1960.

Dear Surena:

Hebrews 13:20, 21
Your letter was such a blessing to our hearts. You are beginning to open your heart to the guiding and teaching of the Holy Spirit! Hallelujah! The things you are receiving are not strange to us. We have believed and taught and practiced this message and

ministry for several years. It may not have seemed so to you, but we must lead the lambs gently along this blessed way of life in the Spirit.

Oh, how blessed to walk in the Holy of Holies and hold sweet communion with our precious Lord Jesus. What a glorious fellowship is ours! An ever-unfolding revelation of His provisions for His redeemed! Glory! Glory! Oh, there is a surge of holy blessedness going through my whole being! There are richer, fuller, nobler, greater things in store for those who are willing to follow Jesus all the way!

The Lord gave us a most gracious outpouring of His Spirit in January. There were 36 filled and quite a number saved. Several new ones are coming and many joined us last month. There were eighteen, I believe.

Earl and Fern Johnson have taken a church in Wilbur, Washington, and are happily pastoring!

You are certainly missed here, even yet. We must say, "Amen" to the guidance of our Lord. Perhaps you will be back. He knows.

May the riches of His grace keep you constantly rejoicing in Him.

Your pastor and brother,

M.J. Stewart
P.S. You will always have a special place in our hearts.

It was a shock to the congregation when Stewarts announced they had accepted the pastorate at Peoples

Church in Ventura. Nobody likes saying good-bye to Christians they love, especially this band of people, but the time had come for the Stewarts. Some of the relationships had been developing since the Stewarts arrived almost ten years earlier. Milton and Ruth felt led of the Lord to give the home they were buying from the Priesses to the church to be used as a parsonage. They signed papers turning ownership over to the church, taking no money from the transaction. Although their work in the city was finished, their influence in the lives of many members continued through the years.

Milton's mother
Myra Norris at age 18

Milton's grandparents,
Milt and Matt Norris

Milton at age 3

Lawrence Barrett Stewart, Milton's father,
playing baseball in the Army

Eugene High School graduation

Milton & Ruth prior to marriage in
front of Lighthouse Temple (1942)

Milton (front left) with Harold Powers
(center) and students of Bible Standard
Training School

Milton and Ruth after a
front door smooch

Milton & Eve Bennett tug-o-war
at Open Bible youth camp

Ruth & Milton with baby Pam (1943)

Martinez church flyer

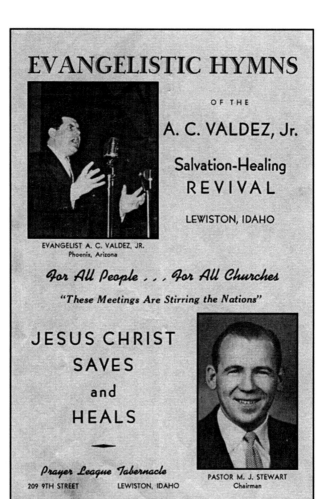

A.C. Valdez Revival flyer (1952-53)

Bill & Ethel Phair with daughters
Lois, Jane, Ruth, Marian (back) and
Josephine (front) circa 1942

Stewart Family, Lewiston, circa 1958

Always a proud Scot!

Lewiston church honors
Stewarts with their first wedding
cake … about 15 years late.

A "love offering" from
Lewiston congregation
brings joy

Pastor & Mrs. Stewart, Lewiston (1958)

Ruth & Milton
A day off at a farm near Lewiston

Pam, John, Ruth, Pat, and
Bobbi Jo at their Lewiston home

Milton and his father, Lawrence Stewart

Praising Him with the trumpet

Milton and his mother, Myra

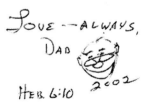

Self-portrait salutation to Pam

Milton & Ruth celebrate 60
years of marriage (2002)

EBC President David Cole and
wife Julie with Milton at dedication
of new chapel (2008)

Milton & Ruth still playing
their instruments at 60th
wedding anniversary

Stewart children, Pam,
John and Bobbi Jo (2008)
(Patty not present)

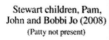

* * *

Chapter Eight

Revealing the Inner Man

"Lord, who may dwell in your sanctuary?
Who may live on your holy hill?"
Psalm 15:1

There was nothing phony about Milton Stewart's spiritual life. If there was one dominant characteristic about him, it was his desire to be filled with the Spirit. This wasn't only a Sunday goal, but a longing to live seven days a week, 24 hours a day, in the power of the Holy Spirit. As a pastor and man of God, he had the spiritual responsibility of his family and congregation. This required his priorities to be in order—giving himself first to prayer and the study and teaching of the Word of God. The business aspects of the church were not ignored, but were secondary.

"I have never, personally, known a man in my life who so lives in the Spirit of God as does Brother

Stewart," said Louis Malmin, a respected Norwegian evangelist who ministered several times in the Lewiston church. Whatever he did for the Lord, it was with wholehearted devotion to Christ, whether to preach, pray, counsel, teach or encourage. It was not that he was driven to pay the ultimate price for the blessing of God, but rather that he had discovered a place to live in intimacy with his Savior far superior to anything human effort could generate. It was a place paid for through the death and resurrection of Christ, given freely, with generosity and grace through the Spirit to His children. He was one of them! This realization motivated Milton to give back to God, in his most energetic manner, his entire life. Living by faith in union with Christ was the norm characterizing Milton Stewart.

When Milton renewed his commitment to Christ, the conviction that the Bible was the infallible Word of God came with the package. This question of the inspiration of Scripture is a crisis point for many preachers of the Gospel; Milton got it right. The preaching of E.J. Fulton and Fred Hornshuh Sr., along with the teaching of Harold Powers and his other Bible college teachers solidified his faith in the verity of Scripture. That God had a plan for his life was not in question, so he was determined the working out of that plan was going to be according to the Book. Preaching the Word, and his allegiance to its directives, would guide both his personal life and his public ministry.

The hollowness within his inner man, partially due to the lack of a father image, was replaced by a hunger to know his heavenly Father and be obedient to Him. God's Word came alive to him as he began to believe and act upon the great promises he was finding in his Bible. Among the core truths that transformed his life were the Scriptures identifying who the believer is in Christ. Since God's Word revealed it, he would believe the truth, live in that belief, and preach it with conviction. A dozen of these life-shaping truths are paraphrased here:

As God's child, I am an heir of God and a joint heir with Christ. Romans 8:17

I am the workmanship of Almighty God. Ephesians 2:10

My body is the temple of the Holy Spirit. 1 Corinthians 3:16

I have been chosen and appointed by God to bear Him fruit. John 15:16

I am a citizen of heaven, seated with Christ. Eph. 2:6; Philippians 3:20

God has given me everything I need through my relationship with Jesus Christ. Rom. 8:32; 2 Peter 1:3; Phil. 4:19

I am more than a conqueror through Christ.
Romans 8:37

The fullness of Christ has been given to me.
Colossians 2:9-10

God loves me just like He loves His own Son.
John 17:23

God's anointing on my life continually abides
in me. 1 John 2:27

When I am obedient to God, He discloses
Himself to me. John 14:21

My worship and praise of God prepares my
heart for His blessings. Psalm 50:23

It would be difficult to have been under the
influence of Milton's ministry and not absorb these
marvelous truths of God's Word. He often said that
God has a plus sign beside every promise in the
Word. Our part is to say "Amen" to His promises
and act upon them (2 Corinthians 1:20).

Jesus promised his disciples, "the Holy Spirit will
teach you all things and remind you of everything
I have said to you" (John 14:26). Having a surface
knowledge of the Word of God would never satisfy
Milton. His prayer life was inextricably intertwined
with the study of the Word. When kneeling in prayer,
more often than not, his Bible was open before him.
God's Word was alive in him, the eternal and present

message of God. He would often say, "This Book is more up to date than tomorrow's newspaper." Some people may call it an eccentricity, but he would never place another book on top of his Bible at home or church. It was not a fetish or "bibliolatry," but a personal conviction, seldom uttered. Those close to him were aware of the practice. If God honored His Word and His Name above all things (Psalm 138:2), Milton would show respect for God's Word. Not only was Christ first place in his life, but His Word was also the dominant book driving his life.

During the summer of '54, Del Storey came home from Bible college, along with a number of other students from Lewiston. Del was a bold, outspoken and visionary young man with obvious leadership skills. There was some talk about Del and Brother Stewart getting a tent and holding revival meetings wherever the Lord would open doors. There were no concrete plans, but the two men had a vision for the lost and a desire to be used of God. They announced to the congregation of Prayer League Tabernacle that they were going on a fasting and prayer retreat to seek God's will for their future.

When they returned, Milton told a bit about their times of prayer, then stated what he felt God had solidified in his heart. "Although we received no clear word from God about our future ministry, I came away from our retreat with one inner conviction. It was not an earthquake or a thunderclap revelation from heaven, but a familiar conviction in God's still, small voice encouraging me to believe

God's Word. God has given all the revelation we need in His Book, and before and after any climactic experience we could imagine, He simply wants us to believe Him and put into practice what He says." The Scripture was the centerpiece around which his ministry would revolve.

His habit of prayer was characterized by regularity, spontaneity, and earnestness. He was always ready to pray, whether in his private life, or with anyone in need. Ruth and Milton's home was open for needy ones desiring prayer. It mattered not whether it was a church board member, a down-and-outer off the street, or one of their Nez Perce Indian friends from Kamiah. Ruth and Milton's lives were characterized by Eph. 6:18, "And pray in the spirit on all occasions..."

Milton's great desire to know Christ and be used by Him kept him in that wonderful place of intimacy in prayer. He loved the Lord and desired oneness with Him; it was a special place where he could communicate with God, and God with him. His place of prayer gave him proper perspective on his ministry and life. If you measured the daily time Milton spent in prayer, it would not be in terms of minutes, but of hours and parts of days and nights. "You don't learn to pray by reading books on prayer," he often stated, "but by praying." He backed up the statement in his lifestyle.

Ruth has been a partner in Milton's spiritual life, keeping prayer lists, which are legendary. Every day there are dozens of people and circumstances she lifts to the Lord in prayer. Her children tell how she will spontaneously pray for people she notices as they are driving down the road. Many are among the most unlovely, but she blesses them, asks God to forgive their sins, and bring people into their lives who will share the Gospel with them. Milton and Ruth have always been a team in ministry, but their united prayers have been the glue that held it together.

Milton's inspiration for maintaining a thriving prayer life came not only from contemporary men of prayer, but from Christ and the apostles. Jesus "offered up prayers and petitions with loud cries and tears to the one who could save him" (Heb. 5:7). Our Lord often went out to a lonely spot and prayed, sometimes spending the whole night in prayer. His disciples asked Him to "teach us to pray," not "how to pray," but "to pray." After the coming of the Holy Spirit, the disciples gave their "attention to prayer and ministry of the word" (Acts 6:4). The most crucial question every minister must answer is "How can I best use my time?" Milton, early in his ministry, determined to live in the power of the Holy Spirit, and that could only be done through an energetic prayer life. Central to his prayer life was the hard work of daily submission to the will and purposes of God.

Prayer time with members of his congregation took place each week. After his Sunday sermon, Pastor Stewart would often open the altar area for people who wished to pray. He would then dismiss the congregation, go to the altar, and pray for those seeking the Lord. He was gentle in approaching those praying, and often would simply ask an individual, "How can I best pray with you?" His heart was full of love for his people, and it would be impossible to know the eternal work done in hearts as he ministered. It never stopped at that point. The needs of individuals were carried into his private prayer life. If Milton or Ruth Stewart told you they would pray for you, you could go to the bank on their word.

It is a beautiful thing to listen to Milton pray. His prayers are more sung than uttered, and those petitions are surrounded with his praise and affection for God and His Word. If you were at the church during the day, you could often hear him in the prayer room or in his office raising his voice to God in praise, adoration, supplication, and intercession. He understood prayer in tongues was not meant to be simply an ecstatic experience, but an opportunity to allow the Holy Spirit to pray through him in exalting the Lord and edifying his own spiritual being. He could echo Paul's testimony, "I thank God that I speak in tongues more than all of you" (1 Corinthians 14:18).

The character qualities emphasized in Jesus' teaching were matters of the heart. It can be instructive to see these qualities in Milton's life through the radical teaching of our Lord Jesus in the first four beatitudes of His Sermon on the Mount. This "blessed" man is a believer who is reaping the favor of God and the respect of those who know him best. His first characteristic is to be "poor in spirit." Putting to rest the carnal man and living in the Spirit was a daily function of Milton's prayer life. The temptation to be exalted in his own eyes, or the eyes of others, had to be tempered by Paul's declarations that "I know that nothing good lives in me, that is, in my sinful nature" (Romans 7:18), and, "I die every day—I mean that, brothers—just as surely as I glory over you in Christ Jesus our Lord" (1 Corinthians 15:31). Listening to him pray in private, for he prayed out loud about nearly everything, made one aware of how seriously he took this admonition.

The second beatitude, "Blessed are those who mourn," is difficult for some to understand. Milton adopted God's worldview of life as his own, and was continually aware of the eternal conflict between good and evil. If Jesus was "a man of sorrows and familiar with suffering" (Isaiah 53:3), should Milton not likewise care and be burdened for those lost and blinded by sin? He also grieved over the daily battle he faced with his own fleshly nature. Because he appeared so happy and full of life, it is difficult for many to see Milton in this way, but there was always an underlying gravity in his life which did not allow him to be frivolous and caused him to evaluate his relationships and responsibilities in the light of eternity. This seriousness was born in his devotional life.

"Blessed are the meek." There is hardly a word more misunderstood than "meekness." Two people about whom this word is used are our Lord Jesus (Matthew 11:29) and Moses (Numbers 12:3). Vine's *Expository Dictionary of New Testament Words* gives the following insights. Meekness is "an inwrought grace of the soul...it is that temper of spirit in which we accept His dealings with us as good, and therefore without disputing or resisting." Milton felt deeply the pain of rejection, the confusion of being misunderstood, and all the hurts associated with living on this troubled earth; but he saw meekness as surrender to his heavenly Father in whom he was fully furnished with all His power and riches. Meekness was not weakness, but strength in the knowledge God was working out everything in his life for His glory.

"Blessed are those who hunger and thirst for righteousness, for they will be filled." The test for this verse works both ways. If Milton was hungering and thirsting for the righteousness of God, he would be living a life filled with His Spirit. By the same reasoning, if he were living in and being filled with the Spirit, it was proof positive he was hungering and thirsting for Christ. David put it this way in Psalm 42:1, "As the deer pants for streams of water, so my soul pants for you, O God." The great inward motivation of Milton's life was voiced by Paul: I want to "be found in him, not having a righteousness of my own that comes from the law, but that which is through faith in Christ—the righteousness that comes from God and is by faith" (Philippians 3:9).

Few people have been more wholehearted in hungering and thirsting for God's righteousness than Milton. It was this passion for God's presence and favor that kept Milton growing and maturing throughout his life of ministry. The applause and honors of men were meaningless without the knowledge that Christ truly was Lord of his life. Year after year, Milton could say with the apostle Paul, "I press on toward the goal to win the prize for which God has called me heavenward in Christ Jesus" (Philippians 3:14). The remaining beatitudes, not commented upon, are also amply reflected in Milton's life.

Praying for the sick and needy is fraught with many potential problems. Well-meaning critics have said, "Think of the false expectations you raise when you proclaim that Christ can heal the sick today." Stewart reasoned, if Jesus Christ is "the same yesterday, today and forever" (Hebrews 13:8), then He can and is willing to answer our prayers right now. Since Milton never read of the apostles and prophets saying "if it be your will, Lord" before praying for the sick, he would simply ask God to answer his prayer right then, and leave the results to the Lord. After all, if anyone experienced a miracle from God, whether physical or spiritual, it was God doing the work. Milton was only His messenger.

There were times in Milton's ministry when a prophetic word to an individual would bring both healing and salvation. Mrs. Gano, the grandmother of my friend, Chuck Jones, had been involved in a religious cult. She came to Lewiston one weekend for surgery on a growth behind her esophagus, scheduled for the coming Monday. She accompanied Van and Alice Jones and family to church. After the service was over, God spoke distinctly to Milton. He went to Mrs. Gano and said to her, "If God heals you of that growth, will you give your heart and life to Jesus Christ and fully live for Him?" She thought for a short time, then answered, "Yes, I will!"

Pastor Stewart did not pray for her, but left her with the decision she had made. That night as Van and Alice Jones were sleeping, Mrs. Gano was making a commotion. They awoke and found her shouting out, "It's gone, it's gone, it's gone...the preacher said it would be, and now it's gone!" She kept her appointment with her surgeon, telling what had happened. He did a thorough exam and informed her she would need no operation because he could not find the tumor. Several years later, Mrs. Gano was killed in an auto accident. When the Joneses went to her home to take care of her personal effects, they found her Bible opened on her bed where she had obviously been kneeling in prayer.

Whether it was training disciples, evangelizing in other countries, or drawing churches together for the work of the Gospel, Milton Stewart was in the middle of the action. His leadership was reflected in Solomon's proverb, "Where there is no vision (inner revelation) the people cast off restraint" (Proverbs 29:18). Among the ministry responsibilities Milton held throughout his lifetime were music minister, song leader for evangelistic services, camp speaker, missionary, evangelist, pastor, radio minister, district and regional superintendent, Bible college teacher, and national board member of the Open Bible Churches. As he matured in his ministry, his heart burned to pass on to others the vision God had given him to evangelize the lost and equip the saints of God.

Wherever he ministered, one of the first things he did was personally visit every church pastor in town who preached the Gospel, and let him know of his willingness to work together with that pastor in common causes of evangelism and ministry. In citywide evangelism efforts in Lewiston, Idaho, he helped with the Hyman Appleman revival tent meetings, and the following year he strongly supported the T.W. Wilson meetings of the Billy Graham Evangelistic Association. Youth for Christ gained a solid foothold in the area largely due to his support and work on the board of directors.

In the early 1950s, there was a significant move of the Lord within Lewiston's Prayer League Tabernacle, and later at the newly formed Open Bible Church. This work of the Spirit of God led a large number of young people and young married couples to prepare themselves for a life of ministry by enrolling at Eugene Bible College in Eugene, Oregon. The life impact of Milton and Ruth Stewart has motivated great numbers into gospel ministry: pastors, missionaries, Bible teachers, Christian school leaders, and their spouses serve God within and without the OBC family because of his influence. Their number has been multiplied in children and grandchildren who have been called to take up the torch, faithfully communicated through the ministry of the Stewarts.

One such person was Joan Davis, a well-known and beautiful young lady from Lewiston with incredible vocal talent. She was working for Washington Water Power in late September when Milton Stewart walked into her office. He knew Joan needed to be in Bible college, NOW! Not later. He greeted Joan, put an application to EBC in front of her and said, "Joanie, you might change your mind, but God does not!" With that he turned and walked out.

The abruptness of his message left her angry, but within thirty minutes, she received a phone call from two Lewiston girl friends enrolled at EBC. These girls had found a perfect apartment to rent, but needed the third person. Would she come? It didn't take her a minute to commit herself to her friends, and informing her supervisor of her need to go to college now, she submitted her resignation. Her supervisor accepted it, and Joan was given both an invitation to return to work there, and also a most favorable letter of reference for future work possibilities.

It was at EBC she met tall, good-looking Del, married him and spent a lifetime in ministry. They raised a family, which is today prominent in the service of the Lord. Significantly, Del and Joan spent their honeymoon directing Vacation Bible School with Stewarts at the Lewiston Open Bible Church.

Milton learned having a vision for ministry meant very little if it was not accompanied by discipline and obedience to the day-by-day work of the Holy Spirit in his life. Equipping workers for the great harvest of the Lord was his heart's passion, and the promise that God would "give him the desires of his heart" encouraged him to direct young people toward Bible school for life preparation.

Early in his ministry, Milton learned to hear the voice of the Lord, not only through prayer and the Word, but also through the inner voice of Holy

Spirit that was very specific. As he obeyed God and communicated accurately what the Spirit was telling him, he grew in confidence. He walked in the assurance God would honor this *rhema* in performing His will. Many who have worked with Milton have testified that when he said, "God spoke to me," he was not blowing smoke.

Wearing the mantle of a prophet was not an office Milton sought; it was clear the message of God's word through his ministry flowed from the intimacy of his relationship with the Lord. Jesus said, "Whoever has my commands and obeys them, he is the one who loves me. He who loves me will be loved by my Father, and I too will love him and show myself to him" (John 14:21). In order to continue to hear God's voice, Milton must be obedient to the Lord's commands. There were times when he had to deliver an unpleasant message from God to an individual. At one crucial point he responded to the Lord's directive, "Lord, I can't deliver that message!" The Lord's reply to his inner man was, "Do you want me to lift my anointing from your life?" Milton's response was to be obedient to his Master.

Max Harris stood with Pastor Stewart outside the doors of the Open Bible Church in Lewiston following the evening service. He was a young high school student who had been visiting the church for a few weeks. He looked over at Pastor Stewart, then began talking in a very negative way about the things of the Lord.

While he was talking, God spoke a word to Milton. He turned to Max and said, "Max, what would you think if we went back into the church and told the congregation what you had been doing this afternoon?" Max was stunned. His face turned ashen and he quickly found a way to leave. A few weeks later, Max was at the altar giving his heart to Christ. He lived a strong Christian life, raising a godly family, and having an effective witness among fellow workers at the post office.

Milton often preached in Edmonds' Open Bible Church at the request of pastors Bill and Karen Clemons. One Sunday he was preaching in the aisle of the church when the Lord directed him to stop and speak a prophetic word to a man seated nearby. This he did, but unknown to Milton, the Lord had spoken earlier to this gentleman saying, "When Brother Stewart comes, he will prophesy over you." The word the Lord gave Milton was that this man would be starting a business, and God would bless him, making him successful. It came to pass as prophesied.

"Are you winning the lost?" Fred Hornshuh Sr. would often close his letters to Milton with this question. Hornshuh was not only one of the original founders of the Open Bible Standard Churches, but in Milton's eyes, his ministry was apostolic in function. In addition to founding several of the most significant Open Bible churches on the Pacific coast, he constantly encouraged pastors he mentored to win the lost. Milton can still picture him at his desk, with his large mechanical typewriter in front of him, pecking out his unedited letters.

Fred Hornshuh's son, Fred Hornshuh Jr., was a classmate of Milton's, and like his father, a soul winner throughout his life. Now in their later years, he and his wife often minister in song and testimony to the elderly in rest homes near his residence. God has so blessed his life of witnessing, he seldom sees a day go by without having led one person to salvation in Christ. The Hornshuh family's testimony in soul-winning has been an encouraging example to the Stewarts.

Milton shares the same soul-winning passion. Throughout his life, he has consciously made it a point to develop relationships with people with whom he did business. Shopping in the large super stores may have saved some money, but Milton has always desired to get to know the store owners and build lasting relationships with them. After trust was established, he would prayerfully ask God for opportunities to witness. His approach to them was full of care and love; any sense of condemnation emanating from him would certainly close doors.

The toughest people to receive our witness are often those within our own family. Milton's father, Lawrence Stewart, might have been rejected by his embittered son because he left the family when Milton was only two. Milton and Ruth took the high road, and from their hearts forgave him. They befriended and witnessed to him throughout his life. In his nursing home, a few days before he passed away, they had the privilege of leading Lawrence to saving faith in Christ.

Robin was the only one of Lawrence's daughters with whom Milton was acquainted. During a summer visit, Milton took her on a drive through the country so they could talk; he shared with her his personal testimony. Reasoning with her about a new life she could have in Christ, Milton asked her if she wished to commit her life to the Lord, as he had done. She was willing, and they pulled off the road to pray together. It was the last time he saw her. She was drowned in a swimming accident later in the summer.

Milton's mom Myra was never open about her faith. Even though there were evidences God had softened her heart, she refused to talk about it with anyone, especially her family. Ruth visited her at the nursing home and while Myra was napping, she happened upon Christian literature Myra had obviously been reading. When she awoke, Ruth asked her about it, but got a snappy reply. The Stewarts saw some changes in Myra before she passed away, and believe God did bring her into His kingdom.

The exuberance of Milton's outward ministry has been balanced by his inward devotion to the Lord Jesus. The flow of ministry comes directly from rivers of living water Jesus promised through the Spirit. The priority of staying "poor in spirit" has been evident to all who know Milton. One of his frequent prayers has been, "Lord, let me be humble enough to always be heard before Your throne." The third verse of the beloved hymn by Elizabeth C. Clephane, "Beneath the Cross of Jesus," sums it up.

*I take, O cross, thy shadow, for my abiding
    place;*
*I ask no other sunshine than the sunshine of
    his face;*
*Content to let the world go by, to know no
    gain, nor loss,*
*My sinful self my only shame, my glory all
    the cross.*

* * *

Chapter Nine

A Fruitful Ministry in Ventura

*"Always give yourselves fully to the work of
the Lord, because you know that your labor
in the Lord is not in vain."*
1 Corinthians 15:58

For ten years Ed and Betty Wood diligently
pastored the Peoples Church of Ventura, seeing
many saved and building one of the finest churches
in the area. The Stewarts and Woods had become
friends when Milton preached for two consecu-
tive years at the Southern California Church Youth
Camp. The second summer, following the week of
youth camp, Ed invited Milton to Ventura to minister
on Sunday. This initial exposure at Peoples Church
began a relatively short but fruitful ministry in
Southern California.

When Ed felt the Lord leading him in another direction, he called Milton, asking if he would be interested in pastoring the Ventura church. Though their ministry styles were miles apart, he recognized the godly manner with which Ed and Betty had led this church. After prayer, Milton allowed Ed to recommend him as a candidate for the vacancy at the church. The congregation approved the recommendation. In the early spring of 1961, the Stewarts left Lewiston for Ventura with Pam in her senior year of high school, Pat a sophomore, Bobbi Jo a seventh grader, and John not yet in school.

When he arrived on Monday, he was in for a shock. Five full-gospel churches had scheduled their regular combined monthly meeting for Wednesday, with the new pastor as the featured speaker. He would begin his ministry in Ventura by speaking to this joint assembly of believers, before he spoke to his own congregation. When Milton began to preach, he got excited, and the more blessed he got, the more he went into motion. He ended up running all the way around the inside of the auditorium, preaching as he went. Ruth knew how sincere her husband was, but had doubts this was the right way to introduce himself to his new congregation and the Spirit-filled believers who came to hear him preach. Her fears were not realized. The audience recognized Milton, not as an exhibitionist, but as an anointed messenger of God who proclaimed the Word wholeheartedly.

Moving from a blue-collar community into the affluent lifestyle of coastal Southern California might have been a threat to some, but the Stewarts did not skip a beat. The Gospel they preached was the same Gospel; the Lord they served was the same Lord; and the people's need to be loved, the same need. With wholehearted enthusiasm they entered into their ministry in Ventura, and the love showered upon their new congregation was fully reciprocated. As was their custom, they neither asked about their salary, nor bargained with the church board about any form of compensation. They were there to serve as ministers of the Lord. The church parsonage at 381 Agnus Drive was a comfortable family home nestled on a hill overlooking residential Ventura.

It is impossible to understand Peoples Church without comment on the church board. Ed Wood had gathered a tremendous group of men to lead this congregation. They were of highest integrity, ability, and honor; leaders within the community; men of means who wanted to do the work of the Kingdom of God. In spite of their differences, they worked together harmoniously. Milton had to watch carefully how he expressed any problem to this board; if they felt anything was lacking through their oversight, their initiative would kick in. They might use their own money, efforts, or time, but the bottom line was...it would get done.

The Stewarts began "The Peoples' Pastor," a radio ministry to the greater Ventura community. It was unabashedly "full-gospel" in its presentation. Through this airwave ministry a number of people were filled with the Holy Spirit and led to a deeper life in Christ. A local Baptist church was between pastors, and a number of its members were hungry for a deeper walk with God. A schoolteacher in that church had listened to Milton preach on the radio hearing him say, "Suppose God has something more for you. Are you willing to receive it? If you are, get alone with the Lord and tell Him you are open to anything good from His hand."

The lady went to her bedroom and in simplicity asked God for his very best. She was filled with the Holy Spirit and began to speak with other tongues. She hardly understood what was happening, except she had experienced an incredible transformation in her spirit. She looked up the phone number of the Peoples Church and called. When church secretary Sylvia Whisler picked up the phone, the lady could not speak English, but went on speaking in other tongues. Sylvia finally got through to her that she could come to the church and talk with Pastor Stewart. By the time she arrived, she was in better control of her speech faculties and had a profitable talk with Milton.

After a number of visitors had been saved, it was decided to have a baptismal service but—there was a problem. The church had no baptistery. A company in Oxnard loaned them a large tank, which was delivered to the platform. With plastic and towels spread around the tank, Milton helped new converts up the steps and into the water. With each baptism came a wonderful testimony of God's grace.

One of the delights of the evening was the baptism of the entire Balding family. Mr. Balding was a cement contractor and his two sons and a son-in-law worked with him in the business. Fourteen members of this extended family had been saved. This included all the adults except the father, and a number of grandchildren. It was discovered that evening, however, that Mr. Balding himself wanted to be baptized. Because he hadn't yet made a commitment to Christ, some of those helping with the baptism wished to leave him out, but Milton said to let him come ahead. When he got in the tank, Milton asked him if he wished to receive Jesus Christ as his personal Savior and become a Christian like the rest of his family. He replied, "Yes, I would." He was gloriously saved and baptized.

For years Milton had longed to go to the mission field, but the opportunity and resources for such a trip had never come together. While in Lewiston, he prayed for the West Indies area, especially after a visit by Open Bible Churches' missionaries Minnie Bruns and Margaret Crandahl. He had visions of dark beings attempting to stop the move of the Holy Spirit there. Van R. Jones, a heavy equipment contractor and member of his Lewiston congregation, had given Milton a large tent for evangelistic work. However, with Van's blessing, Milton was led to give the sizable tent to the burgeoning church of San Fernando, Trinidad in the West Indies. While praying about visiting that field, the Lord reminded him of the story in Matthew 17 where the temple tax was paid through Peter's finding a coin in a fish's mouth. God had made Milton a fisher of men, and would provide for his trip through "a gift in the mouth of a fish."

The "gift fish" the Lord provided was none other than Mr. Balding. His family announced to the Stewarts they wished to fund a missionary trip for him and Ruth. A few months later Milton, Ruth, and son John left for the West Indies with Wilbur Duncan, a pastor from Centralia, Washington, his wife, and son. Their itinerary included Haiti, Jamaica, and Trinidad. From start to finish, the trip was an exhilarating, soul-expanding experience.

Mr. and Mrs. Gulick led the Foursquare mission work in Haiti. Their diversified ministry included an exceptional surprise. Mrs. Gulick was a concert organist and, using her amazing abilities, taught these people to sing, and sing, and SING! The Stewarts still had no idea what could be accomplished in a primitive environment through such dedicated people. Many of their Haitian congregation walked for miles to get to the services and practice in their choir. On the opening night of their meetings, the Stewarts were speechless after hearing this choir, made up of people from the most impoverished nation in the world, sing Handel's "Hallelujah Chorus!"

Mrs. Gulick endeared herself to young John by thoughtfully baking his 5th-year birthday cake, complete with bright pink frosting and cockroaches. Those creatures were everywhere, and at the moment Mrs. Gulick was ready to cut the cake, a huge one dropped right in the middle of it. She simply plucked it off the cake and proceeded to cut out the pieces.

In all three countries, evangelistic services were conducted with Wilbur Duncan preaching the Word and the Stewarts assisting with music, prayer, and counsel. God's Word was honored, and many people were born into the kingdom through this ministry team. What a joy it was to arrive in San Fernando, Trinidad, and see the new, magnificent Open Bible Church and congregation! The tent the Stewarts had sent from Lewiston served the missionaries as their portable church during expansion years of great revival and through the construction of their permanent sanctuary.

Missionaries Don and Ruth Bryan, Kaare and Jean Wilhelmsen, Minnie Bruns, Margaret Crandahl, Wanda Moon, Dora Turner, and Bill and Donna Whitlow had faithfully served these people who now numbered close to a thousand. In a few short years the operation of the church would be turned over to the nationals. God would raise up Cecil and Debbie Quimana to pastor the church, build and direct a training school for ministers of the Gospel, and evangelize the islands of Trinidad and Tobago. The Carlyle Chankersinghs continued this great island ministry. Stewarts' first visit began a life-long relationship with the San Fernando church family, setting the stage for several future trips.

Returning to Ventura, the Stewarts continued to see God drawing the people of the area to Christ and the Spirit-filled life. Episcopalians came to his church wanting to know more about this deeper life in Christ. As usual, Milton made an appointment with the rector to inform him of these inquiries. When he greeted the secretary, she recognized his voice and exclaimed, "You're the 'Peoples' Pastor' on our radio. My mother and I never miss your broadcast. We've been so blessed by your ministry!"

Meeting the rector, the two men found they had both pastored churches in Lewiston, Idaho. The Episcopalian pastor took Milton on a tour throughout his large, ornate church, smoking his pipe as he went. Then Milton came to the point of the meeting: "Pastor, several of your members are visiting my church. They are interested in a deeper walk with our Lord. Now I have no intention to steal any of your flock. They belong to this church, but I do have a suggestion. Simply announce to your people that you will be holding a meeting for those who are hungry for more of God. Then invite Dr. Peto, an Episcopalian layman associated with the Full Gospel Businessmen's Fellowship, to come and talk to this group of hungry believers."

The rector did not think well of Milton's suggestion. "We don't feature those kinds of things here in this church!" he curtly responded. Peoples Church was greatly enriched through the addition of many Episcopalian people and spiritually hungry denominational seekers.

A religion class at Ventura College began discussing the miraculous and teachings on the Holy Spirit coming from Peoples Church. Milton was asked to visit the class as a guest speaker with 40 minutes to explain these teachings and answer questions from the students. Some wanted to set him up for embarrassment through the questions they asked, but Milton simply shared with the students some miracles recorded in the Bible, and what he had seen God do through his ministry. So great was the interest in the subject matter, the class went on for over two hours. When they finally dismissed, one student followed Milton to his car, and as he got in, the young man leaned forward asking him, "Will you pray for me that I may receive this baptism of the Spirit?"

There was a wonderful move of the Holy Spirit through the church as the Stewarts ministered and loved the people. That bond of love and trust grew as the Lord expanded his ministry. People were filled with the Holy Spirit, grew in the Word, and continued looking for opportunities to expand their outreach. Some members heard about an elderly couple that was taking orphans off the streets of Tijuana, Mexico, into their small ranch south of the city.

The men of the church made a trip to look over the needs of this couple. They were being swamped with children and had nowhere to put them. The men pooled their money and bought the family's ranch. By hiring extra staff and building larger quarters, the complex eventually sheltered 93 orphan children. But where would they ever get the supplies needed for so many? The men spread the news of the children's needs through the towns of Ventura and Oxnard, asking retailers for help. The Navy loaned a large truck which they filled with appliances, beds, toys, and clothing. So much was donated by the generous people of Ventura, the men of the church had to rent a warehouse for storage. What a happy sight when they pulled up at the orphanage ranch and began unloading goodies for those children!

When Milton accompanied them on one of their trips, he was told of a brother and sister who had been brought in recently. They had slept every night under the boardwalks of downtown Tijuana. When roused out of their sleeping quarters, they growled and bit those trying to evict them. They lived more like animals than humans. The orphanage director brought these two in and set them on Milton's lap. It had been only a few weeks since they experienced the love and security of this new home, but Milton felt an incredible love for the siblings as they chattered away to him in Spanish. My, how his heart was touched by the children! He followed their lives and was told the boy had become an attorney and his sister a schoolteacher.

Several people from the Ventura church began responding to God's call through Ruth and Milton's ministry. Included are Charles and Carole (Hughes) Miller who have worked in revival groups in the central Willamette Valley of Oregon, and Fayth McConnell and her husband, missionaries to Mexico. In every place the Stewarts ministered, they made an indelible impact upon individuals.

Several families forged lasting relationships with the Stewarts through ministry to their children. Mrs. Trissler was an extraordinary woman with great imagination and passion. Professionally, she directed a children's television program for a number of years out of Los Angeles. She was the creative director of the church's Daily Vacation Bible School program, and it was there young John Stewart first committed his life to Jesus Christ.

The Vittitos treated Bobbi Jo like the daughter they never had; Elva Smith encouraged her in sewing and learning cooking fundamentals; Ethel Feyma mothered her like one of her own. It was hard on the whole family to even think about leaving these wonderful people, but God was beginning to stir Milton's heart.

Although Peoples Church of Ventura was not affiliated with OBC, they had regular connections with the organization through youth camps, district meetings, visiting missionaries and evangelists. While pastor, Milton Stewart had been elected superintendent of the Southern California Open Bible Churches' District, and in that position was aware of the condition of all OBC churches in the Pacific region. His home church, Lighthouse Temple of Eugene, Oregon, was now looking for pastoral candidates. It had gone through several lean years, was depleted in numbers and was a far cry from the thriving church Milton remembered during his years at Bible Standard Training Institute.

When Milton went to prayer in his morning devotional times, he found himself drawn to pray for Lighthouse Temple. The burden wouldn't go away. He heard of good men he knew who intended to apply, then backed away. After several weeks of talking the matter over with Ruth and praying with her, he finally submitted his name for consideration. Traveling to Eugene, he preached a service, then returned to Ventura. Lighthouse Temple contacted him that week with the news the congregation had decisively voted him in as pastor.

The Stewarts' decision to leave Ventura to pastor Lighthouse Temple in Eugene greatly saddened the church and board. Out of their heavy hearts, the board discussed with the family a number of incentives if they would reconsider and remain as pastors with them. When it became plain the decision was based upon God's call to their hearts and was not optional, each board member came to his office, prayed and wept with Milton, and left him a personal memento as a love gift for the family. Only God's distinct call could have pulled the Stewarts away from such a gracious body of believers.

* * *

Chapter Ten

Glimpses of Family Life

"The righteous man leads a blameless life;
blessed are his children after him."
Proverbs 20:7

While living in Lewiston, once a year Ruth would take a personal vacation from her husband and three daughters to visit her family in Springfield, Oregon. During the week she was gone, Milton would begin cleaning the house. It was not an ordinary cleaning, because Ruth and the girls kept the living room spotless for any special person from the congregation who may drop in. This cleaning was by a man possessed — "Mr. Clean" personified in Milton himself. Every piece of furniture was moved, and then cleaned inside and out. Linoleum and hard-wood floors were scrubbed and waxed; windows were washed inside and out. All appliances sparkled when he finished. Then came the coup de grace.

He had excellent tastes, and knowing his wife and current styles, he went shopping for a new outfit befitting the "Queen" of their household. When Ruth arrived home to her spotless house, there in her closet was a new set of clothes including shoes, bag, and gloves. The love and respect he displayed toward his wife created a lasting impression on their girls. But Milton certainly wasn't beyond playing pranks on his wife.

One evening, Pam and her dad were cleaning the house. It was late and when they went into the master bedroom, Ruth was asleep, snoring loudly. Milton had been touching up a number of the lamps with gold finish and a small brush. They took the lamp out of the bedroom, touched it up, and returned it to the lamp stand. It was at that moment an interesting challenge went through Milton's mind. Was his wife sleeping soundly enough he could paint her nose gold without waking her? After all, Ruth loved the gold look! With delicate grace, Milton got the job done and put away his tools. You can imagine Ruth's shock the next morning when she looked at herself in the mirror. It is one of the favorite family memories Pam and her dad share.

Childhood Memories

Contributors: Pam, Pat, Bobbi Jo, and John

As children we had great fun playing the only thing we knew...church. Of course this included weddings and baptisms. With a 1950s crinoline on her head, one layer over her face as a veil, and an ample supply of Mom's collection of sprayed flowers in tow, one of us played the part of the bride. Another sister dressed up in an outfit resembling the groom, and the coveted role of the preacher went to the last girl. The "preacher girl" would look towards the bride and ask, "No, never divorce?" The bride would obediently say, "No! Never divorce." The groom would get the same treatment and answer similarly. Then the preacher would pronounce the couple "man and wife" and add, "Now you may kiss your bride!" Lots of "yuck" to the kissing business, and the ceremony would be over.

Using the piano bench in the living room as our tank, we would solemnly conduct baptismal services. With the new believer standing beside the piano bench, the preacher would say, "I baptize you in the name of the Father, the Son, and the Holy Ghost." The preacher proceeded to bend her poor victim backwards over the piano bench, often dumping her on the floor or hitting her head on the dining room table. After several bumps, a few tears, and a good scolding from the actual preacher of the house, we were finished with our acting for that day.

What's interesting about the PK life is that you don't have only one mother, you have every lady in the church. If you drool, seven women are pulling hankies out of their purses! If you misbehave...Lord have mercy!

When I (John) was about three years old and my folks were pastoring in Lewiston, I had done something that caused my mother to pick me up and start toward the exit. As we were heading toward the inevitable punishment, I'm not sure what went through my little-boy mind, but I shouted out, "Don't beat me Sister Stewart, don't beat me!" You could hear the giggling throughout the congregation.

Dad was the nurturer. When I was in bed with the measles, I remember my Dad bringing me comic books, coloring books, crayons, and music. We had a portable record player and a green metal box of 45s. He would bring them into the room and I would listen to recordings of Mario Lanza, Judy Garland, or Dinah Shore. I still remember every word to Mario Lanza's "The Most Beautiful Night of the Year."

When Grandpa and Grandma Phair came to Martinez to visit Ruth and Milton, they were given the master bedroom, complete with crib and two-year-old Bobbi Jo. During the night, Bobbi Jo was not interested in going to sleep, so she lay awake while Grandpa started snoring. At the end of every breath Grandpa's snoring sound was "shoo...shoo...shoo." When Bobbi Jo had endured it long enough, she stood up in her crib and shouted at her grandparents, "Don't say 'shoo' at me!" She then lay down again in her crib and sang a little song to herself, while Grandma and Grandpa laughed and giggled about their cute granddaughter. Bobbi Jo thought they were laughing at her, and she stood up in her crib again and yelled out, "Shut up, you dumb kids!"

Bobbi Jo was the most adventurous of the girls. Each Sunday morning, after the family arrived at the Martinez church, her mouth was nearly always full of gum. Interesting! One Sunday morning Ruth decided to watch carefully. Sure enough, she saw her daughter lift each seat in the row and pry off enough old gum to give herself a good mouthful.

It was also at Martinez that Pam volunteered her parents for all kinds of things. The church asked to have some meals brought in for a needy family; Pam spoke right up saying, "Mom will burn a meal for you!" Another couple was talking about their difficulties in having a baby. Pam again had the answer, "Mom and Dad will have a baby for you!"

The Trio Years

Music was a huge part of the lives of all members of the family. Each of the children took piano lessons. Other instruments, including the violin and horns were tried, but singing together bridged their growing-up years. Ruth got it started with Pam and Pat singing songs she had arranged for their unison presentation. One day on their way to church, they were practicing in the car when Pat started harmonizing with Pam. She was only three years old, so it stunned Ruth. She turned around and asked Pat to do it again. Pat had no problem doing it again, and from then on Pam sang lead and Pat harmonized. Before Bobbi Jo was old enough to be in school, she joined her sisters, singing the low harmony part. Ruth played the piano for her daughters and worked up the arrangements. It was lots of fun for all of them.

Getting a response from the church audience was quite exciting, especially for Bobbi Jo. One morning after singing, the church gave an especially vigorous applause to the young girls. Bobbi Jo thought if they liked that, she would do something on her own and get a similar reaction from the congregation. She reached over and grabbed Pam's hair, yanking hard enough to pull out a small handful. Later, Ruth noticed Bobbi Jo had some red hair in her hand and asked her daughter, "Where did you get that?" Bobbi Jo replied, "Out of Pam's head!" The reaction she received wasn't exactly what she expected; Ruth and Milton saw to that!

When the family arrived in Lewiston, the girls sang not only for their church services at Prayer League Tabernacle, but also at Youth for Christ rallies on Saturday night. Mrs. Willer in the Martinez church had made Pam and Pat red vests with pleated skirts to match. Now that preschooler Bobbi Jo was singing with them, Grandma Myra bought a little suit with a red jacket so she would match her sisters. Boy, those kids did look sharp! They were an immediate hit at the rallies, and someone hung on them the title "Sweethearts of YFC." Ruth's musicianship shone through every part of their presentation. They practiced to make each song perfect. Her three daughters sang confidently and looked oh-so-cute and precious. Their sound was balanced and the joy of the Lord glowed in their freshly scrubbed faces.

As the girls grew during the ten years they were in Lewiston, Ruth began singing with them, adding a woman's bass part. The sound was now full and mature, a children's group no longer. They never compromised their determination to use their talent only for the Lord. When the family moved to Ventura, the new church enthusiastically welcomed the Stewart Girls' Quartet.

After getting established in the area, Ruth heard of California-wide auditions for young talented groups. The advertised prize all the groups strove for was the invitation to make recordings. She asked her teenaged girls if they were willing to try out. It sounded exciting to them, so practices intensified and arrangements were tweaked as the big day approached. It was thrilling to be on stage with other talented people in something so large as this. Rather than being overawed by their surroundings, the group relaxed and sang as well as they had ever sung. When the auditions were over and the judges' scores completed and reviewed, the Stewart Girls were first-place winners. The family eagerly awaited word about their promised recording opportunity, but the only letter that arrived from this sponsoring agency was news they had run out of money, forcing them to shut down operations. It became a family joke that winning the contest spelled the end of the Stewart Girls' singing group.

Since Pam was completing her senior year in high school, it was inevitable the Stewart Girls would have to change or disband. The Youth for Christ rallies in Ventura relied heavily upon well-known Hollywood personalities, both for their musical entertainment and as speaking guests. Within Peoples Church itself, there was talent galore. The girls were a first-class product, but when Pam left for Eugene Bible College, they made the decision to call it quits. Although Ruth was capable of retooling the parts for a new sound, with their lead voice gone there was a growing reluctance from the remaining daughters to continue. It had been a wonderful ride! The rehearsals, the arrangements, and the people they met! It was a beautiful string of pearls connecting the years and places their family had lived. Some of the most treasured family memories of the girls sprang from the oneness they sensed as they sang together for the Lord.

Household Discipline

For the most part, the girls got along quite well. Ruth and Milton set down rules for the children, which included always speaking the truth, no gossip, no name-calling, and keeping family affairs within the family. Milton's work ethic was probably not as balanced as it might be today. There was no Dr. Dobson, and many of the church leaders he admired like Billy Graham, Oral Roberts, Bob Pierce and others were often away from home, giving themselves fully to their work. Milton similarly left the majority of family training to Ruth. Even on Mondays, which were supposed to be his "off" days, there may be needy people showing up and family plans would be cancelled or postponed to attend their problems. He was occupied in ministry, and Ruth was the administrator/organizer. Much on-the-spot discipline she handled, but a familiar refrain was heard in the Stewart household, "Wait until your father gets home!"

Mother didn't spank the children often, but her strong convictions on the truths of the Bible brought the fear of God into their home in disciplinary matters. When the children deviated from truth, Ruth would get out her Bible and read Revelation 21:8: "But the cowardly, the unbelieving, the vile, the murderers, the sexually immoral, those who practice magic arts, the idolaters and all liars, their place will be in the fiery lake of burning sulfur. This is the second death." When she came to the part about "all liars," Ruth's voice would rise and Pam says she could feel the flames of hell on the back of her legs!

If the children got involved in name calling, Milton's discipline methods became most interesting. He had a continuing fascination with the English language and the meaning of words. One day while Milton was home with his family, Bobbi Jo got caught calling Pat a "brat." This was a banned word from the Stewart household, as were all slang expressions. It could have been that Bobbi Jo's reactive use of the word was in response to Pat's baiting her with the same word; nevertheless, there was parental reaction. When the family sat down for dinner that evening, Bobbi Jo was asked to get "The Webster's." She had to stand at the end of the table, look up and read the meaning of "brat." That dictionary's definition included the word "bastard." When *that* definition was looked up and read aloud, everybody heard the word, "illegitimate," etc, etc. The girls seldom used any of those banned expressions within earshot of their father or mother. Today's definition in Webster's is mild compared to the 1950 edition. One interesting outcome of this discipline became the whole family's life-long fascination with words, their meanings and uses.

Pam can recall only once when she was spanked as a child, but that incident also included the other two girls. The scene was in the sanctuary of Prayer League Tabernacle when Pam was in junior high school and her sisters a year or two behind. One of the cardinal sins to avoid was gossip, and the girls had been warned more than once that talking in a negative way about others was unacceptable. A young girl in the church developed a quick, but fervent crush on the son of evangelist Miller who had come to minister at the church. The Stewart girls overheard her singing the familiar chorus, "I Love Him Better Every Day." This girl, however, inserted the name of evangelist Miller's son into the song she sang, doing the slow "bridal march" as she walked down the aisle The girls were laughing at her with some teasing over her exaggerated stepping down the church aisle. Someone overheard the whole affair and reported it to their parents.

The kids knew they were in trouble. Pam got it as bad, or worse, than the others, because, as the eldest, she had set a poor example for the other girls. While dad was spanking Pam, mother entered the room and said she thought they had all been punished enough. The lesson was well learned.

John only recalled one spanking he received from his father. The tools hanging in the garage at their

Ventura home were off limits to John. He was not to take them down or play with them. However, John saw his father out working in the yard, and wanting to be a good helper, determined to get the rake down from the wall. At six years of age, John didn't have the strength to keep the head of the rake in balance as he lifted it from the wall. The top-heavy rake fell on top of their car, leaving a row of dents. When Milton heard the whole story, he was in a quandary. His son's motivation was unmistakable, but he had been disobedient. He went ahead and spanked his son, but through this correction he cried and apologized, reminding John that the punishment was for disobedience, not for wanting to help.

Getting Along

Some people feel preacher's kids are a bit special, and have fewer problems than others. That simply is not true. There were wonderful times, and there were also some pretty dark days. In the early years, the girls had normal squabbles and disagreements, but got along with one another quite well. Since they were close in age, competitiveness cropped up occasionally. Pam, being the eldest daughter, was often put in charge of her younger sisters. She made sure everyone was accounted for and often served as the mediator between Pat and Bobbi Jo. Because Pat was the middle daughter, her mother often cautioned Pam, "Be sure Pat gets treated the same as you and Bobbi Jo."

It seemed Pat and Bobbi Jo always had to share a room. They might be in bed for the night, but then they would burst into song, burp the alphabet, and see who could make the funniest sound. This was tough on Ruth and Milton, whose bedroom was directly above the two girls. He would grab a shoe and pound it on the floor as he hollered, "You girls go to sleep." At this threat, Pat would break into uncontrollable giggles. Before long, Bobbi Jo was laughing too, and that always brought further shoe thumping. The girls would quiet down for a moment, and then begin to lightly whisper. When the whispers turned to a roar, so did Milton. It usually took three rounds before the girls were silent for the night.

In their first house in Lewiston, the girls played on top of their detached garage roof. Once Pam and Pat had a disagreement about something, so Pam simply gave Pat a shove. Off the roof she flew, onto a large lilac bush that broke her fall. Well, no harm, no foul. Pam doesn't remember being spanked for that one. When the teen years came, the area of worst conflict was over borrowed clothing. It was usually OK if you asked ahead and didn't presume your sister would approve.

A completely new dimension was added to the family when John was born. He was almost exactly ten years younger than Bobbi Jo, the youngest daughter. Rather than being jealous of this newborn entering their family, Bobbi Jo considered him her own real live doll. She adored him. After he turned one, she often would set him on her lap in the rocking chair and read nursery rhymes to him. John would turn pages too fast for Bobbi Jo to finish a verse, so she memorized the entire book of Mother Goose nursery rhymes. John could now flip pages while she recited the verses. The one conflict she had with John was over birthday parties. Their mother thought it would be fun to celebrate John and Bobbi Jo's birthdays together. After two years, Ruth recognized that sharing the day was not appreciated by her children. From then on, it was separate parties and any spats of jealousy were gone.

With his sisters so much older than he, John often felt a bit like an only child, especially when the girls finished high school and moved from home. His last ten years with his parents were without the presence of sisters. Pam had mothered him; Pat had spoiled him rotten—spending the entire first paycheck from her first job on him; Bobbi Jo and he finally grew up enough to agree that sharing a birthday together was not a bad idea after all.

The common bond of music was a special gift for all the children. When John lived in Ventura, he began playing the piano. He would sit at the keyboard with legs dangling (he couldn't reach the pedals) and plunk out Sunday school songs. One day as he was sitting there, Ruth came by and stood watching with amazement as her son played and sang. It all seemed so natural to John. He could hear the music in his head, and his fingers found a way of matching what he heard. He began lessons shortly afterward and continued music and piano lessons through high school. At Winston Churchill High School, he began working with brass instruments, learning to play the baritone, trombone, tuba, French horn, and trumpet. In later years, John had become accomplished enough on the piano to accompany his mother on her violin.

Pat had more natural talent in music than her sisters. Once she learned the basic scales and key signatures of the piano, she was off and running. It was frustrating to Pam and Bobbi Jo to spend hours in practice, then watch their sister, with no practice, fly through the same piece of music without a flaw. In addition, Pat learned to play by ear, so if she heard a song once, she could sit down and play it on the piano. The same was true on the violin. It didn't take her long to master the basics and even play with vibrato.

Pam, who always carried the lead part in their trio, has enjoyed solo and choir music throughout her life. The pleasure of singing, both as a part of worship and as sheer fun, has remained a most satisfying activity in her life.

Helping One Another

The Stewart family was a unit; if one member hurt, the others pitched in and helped out. Sometimes it was for the sake of the kids, but at others, the whole family had to rally around the parents. Some examples:

Pam started the first grade when her parents were pastoring at Martinez, California. In the middle of the second week of school, Pam brought some papers home with her name written at the top right hand corner. It was spelled, "MAP." Milton asked her to write something for him, and picking up the pencil in her right hand, she started across the page...right to left and backwards...hmm. The next day, she was accompanied to the school by her father. The teacher was told, "My daughter is left-handed. DO NOT try to make her right-handed," and the pencil returned to her left hand.

When Milton and Ruth were married, she had never been taught to drive. The girls were fairly small when Milton felt it was time for Ruth to learn. They carry some pretty vivid memories about those days. It would have been a good time to hire a baby sitter rather than having their precious young ones in the back seat. Pam remembers thinking, "This is it. We are all going to die!" Gas pedals, clutch and brake all got confused as they continued to lurch forward, coast backward, buck and jerk—until they were up against the back fence! To this day, when Ruth drives too fast, Milton begins singing, "Nearer My God To Thee." Ruth doesn't think it's too funny, but both of them rejoiced when the automatic transmission was invented.

Following a Sunday evening service at Prayer League Tabernacle, the family had to wait in the church sanctuary while Milton met with the board of the church. Things had not been going well, and the tension in the church was palpable. As the men continued to talk, their voices grew louder and louder. Ruth and the girls were sitting close enough to the office to hear pretty clearly what was taking place inside. Finally, Ruth had had enough! She stood up and told the girls to stay put, because she was going in! That redheaded wife was not going to stand by and allow her husband to be disrespected. The children all heard what she had to say to those men. "My husband has just poured out his heart and soul ministering to this congregation. How dare you sit here and accuse him of these things? None of it is true." There was more said, and even though Ruth's support did not end the conflict, nobody could ever accuse her of being a pushover when it came to supporting her husband and his ministry.

Leaving a Legacy

Our last link in this chapter comes from a question asked each of the children. What do you feel is a lasting legacy your parents are leaving you? The answers were so similar, they are grouped here without personal identification.

The Stewarts have never been wealthy, so there will not be a large monetary inheritance for their children. In giving, they were exceedingly generous, and practiced what they preached. Whenever Milton, as a pastor, was asked to speak outside his own pulpit, if he were given an offering, he would put the offering back into the church he was pastoring. In denominational causes in which he invited others to invest, you could absolutely count on Milton to be one of the first and most generous to give to that cause.

The Stewarts will leave some family mementos that have great personal value. Among them is Ruth's prayer list that Pam asked for years ago. She also knows that inheriting the list means taking responsibility to pray for those on the list. She's happy to do that.

There is, however, a very rich inheritance, indeed—the inheritance of souls, literally around the world. Their passion to bring people into the Kingdom of God, and equip them to reach lives for Christ today will be an enduring legacy wherever the Stewarts are known. There is no way to count the souls that are a part of God's Kingdom as a result of their lives.

In administration, Stewarts taught that people must always come first, then the process. Ruth and Milton considered people and their needs a primary motivation. A program isn't successful if it doesn't meet the felt needs of people!

The Stewarts have always loved people, with all their faults. As unlovely or unlovable as people may be, they were always able to find something in each individual to love and treasure. This is such a gift. Ruth has her little entourage of what may be called "different ones"! She sees value in them and loves them, never giving up on them. They become her little "projects;" people who need special love, care and attention.

Another legacy is in the Stewarts' ability to forgive. They have never harbored resentment toward any who may have done them wrong. They realized early in their ministry that an unforgiving spirit keeps you eternally attached to your offender. The only way you can be truly released from the pain of your own past is through forgiveness. Ruth has been so open about this. Driving down the road, she will notice people on the street and under her breath will pray, "Lord, I forgive them for whatever they've done, and I ask You to forgive them as well."

When Pam was at EBC and wondering what the will of God was for her life, her father gave her one word: "abide." If she would abide in Christ, even though mistakes were made, they would ultimately work for her good, because she lived in Christ.

The Stewarts never seemed to lose their sense of humor, in any situation. They trusted God for everything.

When the Stewarts left Ventura for Lighthouse Temple in Eugene, Oregon, Pam was already enrolled at Eugene Bible College; Pat stayed in Ventura, working in a bank; Bobbi Jo had one year left in high school, which she took at South Eugene High. John, on the other hand, was enrolled at Eugene Christian School. He was a third grader, and on his first day the author remembers the joy we both felt as he began classes in the school I had been invited to lead. Even though there were eighteen years between us, we shared two important things: 1) the same name, which we both love, and 2) the same father, even though Milton was a "spiritual Dad" to me. His life and legacy were as valuable as that of my biological father, also an excellent and godly man. The four or five years John was enrolled at the Christian school helped lend stability to a young man who needed a safe haven for his academic and spiritual growth.

* * *

Chapter Eleven

Regional Cornerstones: LHT and EBC

Lighthouse Temple

*"For no one can lay any foundation other
than the one already laid,
which is Jesus Christ."*
1 Corinthians 3:11

The Stewarts' challenge at Lighthouse Temple (LHT) was enormous. The great revivals of the twenties had established Lighthouse Temple as a center of Pentecostal activity. Being the mother church of Eugene Bible College set it apart as a church of prestige. It had had its ups and downs through the years, but now, the church struggled with a diminished congregation and waning influence in both the Bible college and community.

Many who remained in the church were strong people who hungered for a fresh move of the Lord. Having a pastor whose ministry had been characterized by the activity of the Holy Spirit generated a possibility of exposing the congregation to disorder. Still, congregational worship was always given a prominent place in Stewart's ministry. The first few months, one of the church ladies would deliver a message in tongues and another would interpret. This was done in an orderly manner, but Milton felt the timing of these gifts wasn't right, and newcomers could be turned off by a freedom of worship they did not understand. He asked his wife to talk to these ladies and suggest a special meeting just for "saints." Out of this need for the exercise of the gifts came a Wednesday evening service in the basement chapel designed for believers only.

As these meetings began, they were accompanied by a heightened awareness of the presence of the Lord. All elements of prayer, worship, singing, preaching, teaching, testimonies, prayer for the sick, and the exercise of the gifts of the Spirit were welcomed. People began to fill the smaller chapel, overflowing into the kitchen area. Bible college students, hungry for more of God, left their studies for the evening and became an essential and vibrant part of these services. People were healed, filled with the Holy Spirit, and delivered from the oppression of the enemy. It became a book of Acts' laboratory.

During the Stewarts' second year at LHT, Milton had the privilege of hosting the 40th anniversary celebration of the founding of the church. They invited the church's first pastor, Fred Hornshuh Sr., to be the featured speaker. Many in the community who formerly had attended the church, came back to this celebratory event. It was evident the church had begun to experience revitalization under its new pastor.

With a greater semblance of order in the main services, the congregation began to experience growth again. Milton's preaching style did not change. He preached all over the platform and up and down the aisles. One of his board members who always sat comfortably in the back of the church, was irked by this and challenged him on being too informal. Milton's response was, "You start sitting down front, and I'll stop running the aisles!"

Being a board member in a church setting carries not only a responsibility for the good of the church, but the chance to exert personal power. When there is a clash of wills between board members and pastor, results can be debilitating. A former pastor at LHT had fired the custodian, with good cause. When the board heard of this, they rehired the man over the protests of the pastor. A few months into his new job as pastor of the church, Milton began to see why his predecessor had let the man go. He not only did poor work, but there were serious compromises in his life. When the time for action arrived, Milton had already felt several board members attempting to bully him with their opinions. He recommended the firing of the man, then told the board, "If any of you have the idea you will rehire this man as your custodian, let me give you notice that you have just hired your new pastor!" That Milton would lay his own job on the line over the release of the custodian, sent a clear message to his board. In matters of principle, he would step up to the challenge.

On the surface, the above incident looks like a simple power play between board members and pastor; it was much deeper. Milton prayed earnestly for those in his care, especially men and women in leadership positions. He was not naive, but tenderly conscious of the spiritual maturity, or immaturity, of each individual. Some in leadership roles seemed to be not much more than dead wood needing to be thinned. Still, he loved them and interceded for them. There existed in his heart a dominant love for people, stubborn in its steadfastness. God had "set eternity in the hearts of men" (Ecclesiastes 3:11), and regardless of an individual's condition, Milton believed the Spirit of God could breathe on him until he "came to life," as did the valley of dry bones (Ezekiel 37). Such unguarded love left him vulnerable to hurts. But if his Lord and Master died for him, it followed that he must also "lay down his life for his friends" (John 15:13). His attitude was a reflection of "Outwitted," a little poem by Edwin Markham.

> *He drew a circle that left me out,*
> *Heretic, rebel, a thing to flout.*
> *But love and I had the wit to win,*
> *We drew a circle that took him in.*

Several core people were energetic in moving the church ahead. Among them were Hiram Huffman, Bill Shelley, Phil Shelley, and Dan MacIntyre. When Milton pointed out the outdated and awkward location of the church offices, these men got busy and did some serious remodeling. The offices had existed behind the platform in the southeast corner of the main floor. Using the restrooms meant a trip down the stairs, followed by a hike through the length of the building to the ancient lavatories. The men designed a full make over, re-plumbing and rewiring portions of the 1925 building to accommodate functional new offices and restrooms in the northeast corner. What a blessing for the pastoral staff!

Al Haines was not only a talented and faithful leader of the church orchestra; he was also a man of vision. Why should the world's musicians feast on the riches of outstanding music, but the church be stuck with leftovers? Since he already had several top-flight instrumentalists playing in the Sunday evening orchestra, why not recruit some additional people to fill strategic gaps and have a big-band sound from their group?

With the OK from the church board, Al began writing music and arranging hymns in creative ways, with full orchestration. His talent was amazing. Milton visited Al at his home one day when he had some music to arrange. Laying out the orchestral staff paper, he began filling in notes for all instruments with the speed of someone writing a letter. His expertise stunned Milton. Through Al's enthusiastic efforts, the orchestra, at its height, had five saxophones, clarinets, a bass clarinet, several trumpets, tubas, violins, trombones, percussion and various other instruments, giving it a sound seldom heard in church. To top it off, Al built tasteful music stands with a large "LT" painted prominently on the front, a la Lawrence Welk. In spite of the shock this new music was to some old timers, Milton's strong support of Al's musical vision quelled any opposition. With Ruth directing the church choir, and Desta Swaggart on the piano, it was hard to imagine a better music program in Eugene than the one at LHT.

Milton and Ruth never forgot the wonderful Christians they met in San Fernando, Trinidad. While on a previous trip there, they saw a special need. There was a complete lack of any musical instruments within the church. Steel drums were popular in that culture, but that was not all this church needed. The Lord began prompting the Stewarts to help this mission church. "Here we are," Milton thought, "in our American church with an orchestra full of wonderful instruments, and the Trinidadians are fortunate if they have a single keyboard in their church. What if we were to bring them some instruments?" Milton shared this vision with Al Haines and planning began.

The call went out to the people of LHT for any used instruments they would be willing to donate to the Trinidad church. The manager of the music store directly behind the church was delighted to be a part of this cause. He not only refurbished these instruments to look and sound like new, without reimbursement, but donated several used brass and reed instruments from his store. When the sixteen instruments were boxed and crated, Al paid for shipping, and off they went. The church board felt Stewarts needed to be at the San Fernando church to present this gift to their congregation, so they paid for their trip. Arriving in Trinidad, Milton picked up the crated instruments at customs. That Sunday morning, in front of the congregation, the crate was opened. Milton picked up each instrument, told a bit about it, then gave a personal demonstration to his Trinidadian audience. All sixteen instruments were turned over to the pastor for distribution among his people.

During the decades of the fifties and sixties, gospel quartet music became very popular. The Blackwood Brothers, Stamps Quartet and many others sang to sell-out concerts around the country. A. Don Crawley, a longtime member of LHT, had a number of contacts with gospel singing groups through A. Don Promotions. He scheduled concerts from Portland to Roseburg for a number of years. Working with Milton, Don brought some of the best groups to LHT. In extending an invitation, foremost in Milton's mind was the purpose of the groups. Were they coming to put on a show, or to use their music and personal testimonies as a door to share the Gospel? When Big John Hall was scheduled, Milton didn't know what to expect. John had sung with both the J.D. Sumner and Stamps quartets. He broke away from those groups because he wanted to have freedom to share Christ with audiences, as the Holy Spirit led him. He was a dedicated and anointed man.

It was a Mother's Day evening at LHT, and the auditorium was packed. About half way through the concert, Big John took the microphone and began sharing his testimony. Following his talk, he sang another solo. Waiting in the wings was his musical team, scheduled to come back on stage for more songs. But John had a distinct leading from the Lord. He continued sharing the Gospel with his audience, then gave an altar call. It was not planned, but God was in it. Dozens of people came forward to give their hearts to the Lord and rededicate their lives to Christ. As Milton looks back at his years in LHT, that altar call was a significant turning point of God's renewal in the church and community. The growth at Lighthouse surged. People were saved, filled with the Holy Spirit, and awakened by the Spirit of God.

Soon after Milton arrived at Lighthouse Temple, the pastors of the Oregon district elected him their superintendent. This was a responsibility he had carried in Southern California, and he was happy to serve his fellow pastors in that capacity here. Twelve to fifteen churches stretched across the district from Salem to Medford to Klamath Falls, and over to the Oregon coast. Several times a year the men met for fellowship, district business, prayer, and planning. Harvey Klapstein, regional superintendent, often met with the men, providing oversight on issues affecting the entire Pacific division. Often Milton and Ruth went on the road to visit a single church in their district. The pastoral fellowship and knowledge of individual churches was invaluable to them. It also expanded their prayer ministry as they learned of the burdens of their pastors.

When the Stewarts had to travel by car, they loved to break the monotony of their trip by playing games. One of those was a Scripture game they had begun playing when the kids were quite young. It was designed to stump Dad. Ruth or one of the kids would begin reading from the Bible, and Milton would attempt to locate it for them by book and chapter. Often he would have it before they finished the first verse, and it was rare they read more than half a dozen verses before he had it nailed down. Sometimes the tables were turned on the kids and Ruth, and they were asked to find book and chapter. This little game, replayed numerous times through the years, blessed their hearts with the truth of God's Word. It often put the Stewarts into a worship mode. So as they motored through Oregon, Ruth and Milton were often so enraptured by the presence of God, they spent some focused time with hands lifted in worship to Him—safely pulled off the busy highway. They often imagined, with great sense of humor, what people driving by thought as they observed two adults in the front seat of their car, holding the roof off their heads.

When Milton and Ruth arrived in Eugene the summer of 1964, the church attendees of around a hundred fifty people hardly made a dent in the cavernous auditorium that could seat seven hundred.

By the late sixties, the church was nearly seventy percent filled on any given Sunday morning. More importantly, there was an expectation of the blessing of God. As the church grew, Milton added dedicated young men and women to his staff. Skip and Dawn Ringseth accepted the invitation of Stewarts to serve as assistant pastors. They were a joy to the congregation and received wonderful training under Stewarts.

Academic curiosity was not only a lifetime trait of Milton's for himself, but he loved to see those under his ministry stimulated to dig deeper. Upon their arrival in Eugene, Stewarts immediately became known as strong supporters of Eugene Bible College. It fit perfectly with his intense interest in youth and his desire to promote more formal Bible training. When it came to knowing and preaching the Word, Milton had few peers. But, without a formal teaching background, he could not imagine what may be asked of him by the Bible college. He didn't have a long wait.

Eugene Bible College

"A student is not above his teacher,
but everyone who is fully trained will be like
his teacher."
Luke 6:40

That Milton had a special connection with "his kids" at Eugene Bible College (EBC) is a gross understatement. Back in his years of pastoring in

Lewiston, he would have occasional opportunity to attend conference in Eugene. A tide of anticipation would rise in the many Idaho young people he had encouraged to enroll at EBC. "Brother Stewart's coming!" the Lewiston students would unabashedly exclaim. Skip Ringseth, a year behind the author as an EBC student, was pretty disgusted with this adulation. "So their pastor's coming," he thought. "So is mine. What's the big deal?"

Lynn (Bennett) Stafford was sitting in the classroom waiting for the lecture to start when Milton poked his head in to see if any of his kids were in the room. As he glanced around, Lynn spotted him. Up she jumped. Running to the door, she threw her arms around her pastor, exclaiming, "Brother Stewart!" in a voice that could be heard through the building. Not every Lewiston young person was as emotionally charged as Lynn, but there was genuine love and respect for the man who led them with such love and devotion.

Over the years there were probably hundreds of students who attended EBC, largely through the influence of Milton and Ruth Stewart. Whether you were a summer camper, a teen in the youth group, or a young married couple sensing the call of the Lord to service, the Stewarts would enthusiastically point you toward Eugene Bible College. They may not say to you, as Milton did to Joan (Davis) Lumbard, "This is God's will for you!" but they would certainly let you know it was a wonderful place to explore God's options for your life.

With a school of less than two hundred students, it was like family. Friendships lasting a lifetime often were forged there. No one needed to explain why the school was often referred to as 'Bridal Standard College.' Bible classes were exceptional. They laid a foundation for continued Christian growth and service. Many attended EBC much like a junior college, transferring to four-year schools for further study. Like the author, they look back with fondness at the homelike atmosphere where they learned to study and grow in disciplines needed for success in life.

When Stewarts moved to Eugene in the spring of 1994, Harvey Klapstein was both president of Eugene Bible College and superintendent of the Pacific region. He and his wife, Alys, welcomed them warmly, inviting Milton and Ruth to become instructors at the college. In spite of the additional time commitment needed for his class assignments, Milton was delighted to have the opening to teach these aspiring preachers. For the next five years, his teaching load included Pentecostal Truths, Pauline Epistles, and Acts. Ruth was given a class she grew to love: Prayer Life.

The only difficulty Milton had was getting too wound up. The boundaries of time and coverage of exact subject content were open to change, as he felt directed by the Holy Spirit. He was a preacher at heart, and the truths of Scripture continually inspired him. But students are adaptable, and they learned to sense the moving of the Holy Spirit, as their instructor led them. Milton made the Bible his only textbook. Homework always included key verses to memorize; sometimes there were parts of chapters. It was his conviction that hiding God's Word in their hearts was the single most important thing young people could do to prepare for service in God's kingdom. Two decades later Milton heard Jeff Farmer, then President of Eugene Bible College, speak to the student body. From his heart, Jeff quoted several verses he had originally memorized while in Milton's classes. Those verses and others, like the Christology of Hebrews 1:1-3 and Christ's second coming in 1 Thessalonians 4:13-18, have fed and instructed Jeff for years.

Most of his classes were predictable in the material covered, but Milton knew from John 14-16 and 1 Corinthians 12-14 that the Holy Spirit was given to the church as a teacher who would lead us into all truth. It was not uncommon to turn to worshiping the Lord, and inviting the Holy Spirit's direction within his teaching. Occasionally the gifts of the Holy Spirit like tongues, interpretation of tongues, and prophecy, would be welcomed. The students knew Brother Stewart would lead them firmly in the Scriptures, and a part of real scriptural understanding is experiencing the activity of the Holy Spirit. Having a teacher equipped to lead students through these experiences was a valuable addition to their education.

Milton was pleased when Harvey Klapstein, in 1965, announced the appointment of Ed Wood as president of Eugene Bible College. It would give Harvey more time to concentrate on the Pacific region's business. Milton and Ruth's teaching assignments remained the same except for one needed change— Milton's classes were moved to the basement chapel room. His preaching/teaching style upstairs in a room with paper-thin walls had become a distraction to some other faculty members attempting to teach. Where he taught didn't matter a bit; just turn him loose with the students and he would be happy.

Ruth's Prayer Life class met once a week. Her goal was to integrate teaching of the Word on prayer with actual prayer experience. As in Milton's classes, key verses were memorized. Reading biographies of great men and women of prayer was encouraged, and sometimes assigned. Students were encouraged to express needs, and the class would pray for them. It certainly wasn't a dull experience with Ruth in charge. As students prayed and ministered to each other, Ruth explained how they were filling the role of each part of the body, contributing to the health of the whole church.

One of Ruth's students came to her with a tough problem. This student believed with all her heart that God would meet her needs, but it did not seem to be happening. She explained in detail how she and her husband had made a faith promise to the Lord. They not only did not have the money to fulfill their commitment, but now her husband was out of work. They were broke. As the conversation continued, the Lord spoke to Ruth; she was to empty her purse and give this young lady all her money. Explaining what the Lord had spoken to her, Ruth gave all she had. She later found the girl used the money for her faith promise, but God, in His faithfulness, did supply their needs. As this couple entered the ministry, they became very special friends of Stewarts.

Two students familiar to Milton were the Burke brothers. Larry and Lonnie had been in Southern California camps where Milton had seen their leadership skills as high school kids. He knew how responsible they were and also appreciated the godly family from which they came. As he got more personally acquainted with them in the classroom, he eventually invited both of them to assume responsibilities at LHT. As EBC students, Larry served as the Sunday school superintendent and Lonnie helped as youth director.

This author was a single man in Milton's early years at Lighthouse Temple, and not above a good practical joke. Recruiting a couple of other young men from the Bible school, I talked them into helping me move Milton's little red Renault from its parking place next to the church. That automobile was no bigger than a glorified refrigerator, so it didn't take a lot of effort to get it rolling. With the front door open and several of us pushing, we tried to steer the car out of the parking lot to nearby Hamburger Heaven. Something ran amok, and the door of the Renault wedged against a telephone pole. So, there it was — stuck.

Since I was the instigator of this prank, and we couldn't dislodge the car, it was up to me to break the news to Brother Stewart. When I entered his office, my countenance told him everything. While I attempted to explain, he got tickled. The more I explained and apologized, the more tickled he got. He had never seen me so humiliated before, and it hit his funny bone until he was roaring with laughter. The fact that his car was some damaged was nothing compared to the good laugh he got from watching me grovel. New car doors are expensive! It took two months' of my hard-earned cash to pay for that antic.

W. Ern Bryant, EBC dean of students, was a man of integrity and skill. He developed a warm relationship with Milton, attended Lighthouse Temple and often filled the pulpit when Milton had to be gone. One particular thing Milton admired about Ern...he took notes on all Milton's messages. Here was a man of the Word, highly educated, learning from his sermons. Evidently, from taking notes, Ern discovered a pattern. He approached Milton one day after the service and wryly commented, "Milton, you are the only preacher I've ever heard who has a three-point outline for his introduction."

Milton was often invited to be a guest speaker for chapel services at the Bible college. He loved the honor of preaching there. These were young ministerial and Christian education students, preparing to give their lives to the service of Christ. His anointed messages touched many hearts. While preaching, he would do, in the confined chapel room, what he did at church — walk along the front, down the aisles, sometimes asking questions of students. This intimidated some, and when they found Milton was scheduled to speak, would sneak into a safe seat in the back. This was probably not unobserved by Milton. He and Ruth loved all the students, and it was surprising how many of them the Stewarts knew by name.

Change was coming to Eugene Bible College. Men and women filled with vision and determination could see that without growth and expansion in every way—physically, academically, and spiritually— other Bible colleges and universities would leave EBC behind to wither on the vine. Through the leadership of Harvey Klapstein, Ed Wood, Don Bryan, Clayton Crymes and a supporting cast of hundreds, this impossible dream became reality.

From 1967 through the mid 1970s, Eugene Bible College experienced an amazing transformation. Milton Stewart was involved in this project from beginning to end, but only in oversight. Others carried the hands-on responsibility. The story needed to be told, so we refer our readers to the Addendum, which tells an important part of this miraculous accomplishment.

* * *

Chapter Twelve

Style and Substance
in Preaching

*"...his word is in my heart like a fire, a fire
shut up in my bones."*
Jeremiah 20:9

Phillips Brooks defined preaching as "Truth
through Personality" in his book, *Lectures on
Preaching*. He went on to explain, "'Truth through
Personality' is our description of real preaching. The
truth must come really through the person, not merely
over his lips, not merely into his understanding and
out through his pen. It must come through his character, his affections, his whole intellectual and moral
being. It must come genuinely through him."

In Milton's case I must add, "under the anointing
of the Holy Spirit." For him to preach otherwise
would be little more than sermonizing. His interest
was not in the knowledge he could pass along, but in

the eternal Word being engrafted in the hearts of his audience by the Holy Spirit.

There was boldness and authority in his preaching that left no doubt in the listener's mind that Milton was, using his own expression, "sold out, lock, stock, and barrel." He threw his whole physical being into his presentation...a whirlwind of activity. He was both athletic and acrobatic. Once he started, it didn't take long to have his tie loosened, his coat off, and his sleeves rolled up. No pulpit ever contained him. He was all over the platform, down the steps to the altar space, preaching atop the altar benches, and usually taking a few trips up and down the aisles of the church.

It was as though Milton felt estranged from his audience if he stayed behind the podium. He wanted to connect with his people, see their faces—get in their faces. Whatever it took, he would communicate his message as personally and energetically as he could. His preaching voice was loud and vigorous, matching his physical activity. Whether using a microphone or not, he projected enthusiastically.

Milton's physical expressions while preaching were not a show for effect, but much like the energy of a controlled volcano; the anointed Word of God was simply seeping out every pore of his body. Many have been turned off by the emotionally-charged delivery, only to be gripped by the clarity of the message God was speaking through this man. Milton firmly believed Peter's declaration: "If anyone speaks, he should do it as one speaking the very words of God"

(1Peter 4:11). His mind, heart, and body were united and Spirit-energized in his preaching.

In Milton's first twenty-five years of ministry, he was a special hit at the Open Bible Church youth camps held each summer. He loved young people and their response to him was immediate and enthusiastic. For many years, one week of his summer vacation from the church he pastored was spent at a youth camp, often accompanied by his family. The directors had the whole package with the Stewarts: top class music on trumpet and violin, a man and his family who related well with the teenagers, and a message of challenge and hope hot off the altar of an on-fire messenger of Christ. And for extra kicks, Milton threw in "Bengi," the Bengal tiger puppet who tried to play the cornet. His routine with this little show-off would bring down the house.

On one special occasion, his preaching acrobatics caught up with him. One of the campers, Bob Stafford, recalls the event: "The Lodi district of Open Bible Churches had their family camp at Cazadero near Santa Cruz. Two poles on either side of the platform held the house lights. During the evening service, Milton was preaching enthusiastically all over the platform. He wanted to get closer to his audience so he skipped off the platform, down the steps, and took a swing around one of the poles. His leveraged weight was too much for the lighting system, and the whole thing came down. The lights crashed off and everybody was left in darkness.

"Soon people with flashlights appeared, scrambling around to reconnect those lights, but Stewart kept preaching. Just because it was dark didn't mean he had to stop his message. It took awhile to get order and light back in the service, but it certainly didn't make him any less popular with the campers."

Connecting emotionally with the teens was essential to realizing his spiritual goals. The prayers of the Stewarts and camp leaders were aimed at leading the young people to a saving knowledge of Christ, encouraging them to be baptized in the Holy Spirit, and to be obedient to God's call upon their lives. Whether God called them to missionary work, higher education, or the workplace, Milton pointed out the value of having a biblical foundation at Eugene Bible College.

The camps gave Milton and Ruth an invaluable opening for socializing with their pastor friends, spouses, and camp personnel. The informal gatherings at recreation times and meals allowed them to interact with the campers as well. Many of these relationships begun in camp settings lasted a lifetime.

Milton often preached at Youth for Christ rallies on Saturday night. Word of his enthusiastic style spread quickly, and invitations came pouring in. Ken Brown, a life-long friend, arranged for Milton to speak at a YFC rally in eastern Washington. After he was introduced and began speaking, he found the audience extremely receptive to his message. After awhile, the local director began to worry Milton was not winding down his talk. From the back of the church he gave Milton the sports "time-out" signal.

When he got no response, he walked up the aisle closer to the platform and repeated the signal. Then he went to the other side of the building and did the same. Still no sign of Milton shutting down. In frustration, he finally went to Ken and asked what he should do. Ken told him Milton probably couldn't see his signals, and added, "Just relax, he'll finish when he's ready!"

At another church where Milton was asked to speak, he got a bit long-winded. There was a large clock in the back of the auditorium that a couple of ushers boldly pointed to as Milton preached on. They had no idea Milton simply could not see them. Finally, in exasperation, one of the men took the clock off the wall and replaced it with a calendar! After the service, when Milton was told about this, he enjoyed a good laugh along with the ushers.

The sermons he preached to the young people were challenging, and they sprang from a heart full of the grace of the Lord. Hundreds responded, testifying to changed lives through his ministry. Only heaven can record the eternal decisions made through the ministry of the Stewarts in summer youth camps.

The freshness of Stewart's sermons had much to do with how he prepared to preach. Early in his ministry, Milton was overwhelmed with what he did not know. He was twenty-two years old with middle-aged men and women in his congregation who had walked with the Lord all their lives. He not only felt insufficient, but he knew his grasp of doctrine, general knowledge of the Bible, and skills in working with people were woefully lacking. His ignorance of the Bible and how God worked drove him to prayer and daily preparation for duty in the Lord's kingdom. It became a habit to rise early and spend time on his knees before the Lord. He carried a small New Testament with him for on-the-spot reference. "I always kept my gun loaded!" he would explain.

As he began to preach on a regular basis, Milton developed a style of sermon preparation he carried through life. This thoroughness was evident in his heart-work (on-his-knees time) and his head-work (searching the Scriptures and gathering his background information). He chose a key verse central to his theme, created an introduction to the subject matter, and outlined his sermon in writing, complete with illustrations. When Sunday rolled around, he had gone over his sermon a number of times, and though he always had his outline with him when he preached, he seldom referred to his notes. The message poured out of his heart.

His habits of study, learned and practiced from earliest days in school, carried into his ministry life. There was nothing lazy about Milton. He didn't look for shortcuts to his preparation for Sunday services or for laying the necessary groundwork for a lifetime in the ministry of the Gospel of Christ. He filled his life with books. Biographies of great men of God like Charles Haddon Spurgeon, Robert Murray M'Cheyne, John Wesley, C.T. Studd, William Carey, and many others were eagerly devoured. But the Scriptures were his main diet. Since the Bible itself was its best interpreter, he compared Scripture with

Scripture, studying the context of the verses, examining the author's purpose, memorizing verses and meditating upon them. The Bible was a living document to him, and as a life-long student of the Word, he grew in knowledge and spiritual maturity. His sermons reflected both his deep study and his personal growth.

There were three significant moments in Milton's life when God gave him specific direction in his ministry. The first occurred when he received the baptism of the Holy Spirit in Martinez, California. Beginning to live and walk in the power of the Holy Spirit was revolutionary, and it became his lifestyle. He refused to walk in his own wisdom when the wisdom of Christ was available. Often when preaching, the Lord would blossom a profound thought in his soul that was shared with his audience. It was something he had not thought of beforehand, but which simply flowed from those rivers of the Spirit within him. The miraculous began to take place as he preached. The gifts of the Spirit would operate, both at his direction, and within his congregations. Because God was working, the supernatural in his ministry did not give him pause in his diligent study. The Lord was not about to work through an empty mind and starved soul. In Milton's spirit, there was an expectation that the Lord wished to work His will in every gathering of the saints of God. Since he was a shepherd of the flock, he must be open to the specific, moment-by-moment direction of God's Spirit.

The second of God's messages of direction to Milton took place at the altar during an Open Bible pastors' conference in Southern California. He had made arrangements to make his second missionary trip to the Caribbean Islands; this time he would be the chief speaker. He was nervous about preaching in a culture quite different from the American. He felt very ill-prepared to be an effective minister of the Gospel to these people. As he prayed about this worrisome matter, he heard the Lord speak three simple words to him: "Preach the Word!" His fears began evaporating. After all, preaching the Word was the one thing he really felt confident in doing. Faithfulness in keeping the message of the Word of God central in all his expositions would continue to be Stewart's standard regardless of where he preached.

Following a meeting of Open Bible Church leaders, Milton boarded the plane in Des Moines, Iowa, to fly back to Eugene. His spirit was grieved and deeply troubled. He began to carry on a conversation in his heart with the Lord. Since Richard Nixon was the current President of the United States, he thought, "Lord, can Nixon really speak for America?" As he pondered the question, the Lord began sharing His direction with Milton for a third time. The Lord let Milton know Nixon speaking for America was not a question with which he should concern himself. The important question Milton heard clearly in his heart was, "Who is it that speaks for Me?"

His heart immediately responded, "Lord, I promise never to walk into the pulpit without knowing You are speaking through me." Following that encounter, he became a different man with rearranged priorities. Not only was this a message for him, but for all those who preached the Gospel. He saw his own imperfections and failures in the light of the God of Jonah. After this prophet had fled from the Lord and nearly died in the belly of the great fish, the Scriptures tell us, "Then the word of the Lord came to Jonah a second time" (Jonah 3:1). Regardless of past failures, our God is the God of second chances. God wants to speak clearly again, especially through the ministers of His Word. In Milton's messages and private talks with pastors, he encouraged God's people to be channels He could speak through.

I opened this chapter with a quote from Phillips Brooks, defining preaching as "Truth through Personality." It was evident to Milton that he was not a "regular" preacher of the Gospel. There was an immediacy and spontaneity in his preaching that flew against seminary and homiletic teaching. Questions arose about his style. Why could he not, in the quietness of his study, hear the message of God, organize it and present it in a pleasing format for his audience? Since other ministers of the Gospel were completely different in their delivery, did that make their message of less or more value than his? When criticism over issues of style came from his own minister friends, should he even attempt to make changes to accommodate their expectations of him?

Milton turned to God's Word for his answers. Certainly the value of God's message was not contained in the style of his delivery, but by the Word of God itself, the anointing of the Holy Spirit, and the openness of the hearers. Because the body of Christ was diverse in its parts and functions, so the ministers of the Gospel were gifted differently for the unique purposes of God. When Phillip went to Samaria, as recorded in Acts 8, a large number were converted. He sent for Peter, who came and shared the message of the empowering of the Holy Spirit with this group. Why could Phillip not have done that himself, since numerous signs and wonders had been done through him prior to Peter's coming? Milton could see that every person has been given specific gifts and talents by God, and must exercise them with the strength God makes available. He had to answer to God for how His message was spoken through him. He knew his wholehearted and physical preaching sometimes offended people, but he was not going to sacrifice the day-by-day anointing of the Holy Spirit for a tame gospel message. He would put up with criticism, even from his own ranks, but it was never an easy burden to bear, especially when he became regional superintendent.

Milton had a most interesting question directed at him while attending a Full-gospel luncheon in Portland. The attendees were invited to have discussions at their tables on the topic, "The Present Active Word (*rhema*) of God," or, how does God speak specifically to us today? One of those at his table was a young pastor at whose church Milton had spoken. As they were talking about ministers being used by God in the word of knowledge and similar gifts of the Spirit, this pastor asked Milton, "What is God saying to you right now?" Whether the man was asking the question in seriousness or jest, Milton did not feel he could give an adequate reply.

Later, while driving home, he thought about the broader implications of God speaking to His people. The Word (*logos*) will always be foundational in our faith, but God can also speak to our current circumstances through a specific word (*rhema*). Even the *logos* proclaimed through the apostles in the early church was as different as His leaders were varied. We see obvious examples of the variety of messages in the Scriptures. The seven churches of Revelation received seven very different messages from Christ, through the apostle John. Each of the epistles written by Paul, Peter, James, and John was custom designed to fit a particular church or group of churches. What was needed by that church was delivered through the inspiration of the Holy Spirit to that body of believers. On three occasions, Paul wrote a second letter to a church or individual, which was very different from the first epistle. The same, Milton deduced, is true about a *rhema* spoken to a congregation now. God will work by His Spirit through a pastor or leader to give that body of believers what they need. The Spirit's message to any church or group is what they need at that moment! The key is having a vessel willing to hear and deliver God's message.

Any believer whose heart was open to God, could not help but be enriched by listening to a message preached by Milton Stewart. While preaching, he was that open pipeline to heaven through which God poured out blessing, truth, rebuke, encouragement and hope. If God said, "For where two or three come together in my name, there am I with them" (Matthew 18:20), then God, by His Holy Spirit, would be present whenever we gathered to worship. He would not only be present, He would be active, working, and alive in every believer in the meeting place. That was the premise upon which Milton preached. God would never fail to show up; His messages to His people would be activated by the Holy Spirit in the faithful preaching of His Word.

Milton's sermons were served up in such a practical manner, we could just about eat them. Milton may only cover his "Introduction," but there would be meat, potatoes and dessert available for all.

Some of the most memorable moments with Milton occurred in small groups where he would be invited to share. One morning, while the author was a student at Eugene Bible College, Milton was invited to share with the foreign missions committee. Five of us gathered in the student center of the college for a short devotional. For about fifteen minutes he shared with us the prayer lives of missionaries who had been effective in winning the lost. We'll never forget his stories of Hudson Taylor, Praying Hyde and David Brainerd. What he told of Brainerd was especially poignant. In 1742, after Brainerd had been expelled from Yale for religious reasons, the Presbyterian Church appointed him a missionary to the Indians of Massachusetts. Three years later he lived and worked among the New Jersey Indians. He would rise early in the morning, even in winter, and find a private place outdoors to pray for the salvation and welfare of these men and women. When he finished praying, the snow all around him would be spotted red from blood brought on by the tuberculosis ravaging his body. Brainerd passed from this life before reaching his thirtieth birthday, but left an unforgettable example of dedication to win the lost.

On another occasion, Milton was one of a small group of ministers gathered for prayer. When we finished, we sat around informally and talked about the things the Lord was doing in our lives. Milton opened his heart and shared his great passion and desire to know and be known by his Lord. He illustrated this, referring to the intimacy God designed for us through marriage. "If we are blessed through knowing and expressing our love to our wives, how much greater is it to have the very One who created us, express His love, acceptance, and pleasure in and through us? There exists no greater intimacy than what we can daily experience through our relationship with Jesus Christ."

The life-shaping truths we listed in the previous chapter were common themes Milton expounded upon in his sermons. The "Exchanged Life" principles, which have birthed whole movements, were thoroughly engrafted into Milton's personal life and preaching. Although we will always have, in this life, a fallen nature, we have been given by Christ, His own life. If the Bible were not so clear on this topic, it would be sacrilege to even discuss it. We certainly do not become "little gods," but the Almighty One has chosen to make His dwelling in temples of clay, and that is us. This is the "mystery" which Paul referred to in Colossians 1:27. Christ living in us is "the mystery that has been kept hidden for ages and generations, but is now disclosed to the saints" (Col. 1:26). Milton's sermons around this central theme built into his audience a life-long confidence and maturity in Christ. Milton and Ruth were godly examples of such a lifestyle, and loved their church members unconditionally. The results were an irresistible drawing of people to the magnetic Christ.

Ruth Stewart was not only Milton's life-long wife, she was indispensable to his life and ministry. When a high school girl, God put a call on her life to serve Him as a pastor's wife. For some, being the wife of a pastor exposes a woman to the weaknesses of his life not apparent to the congregation. Ruth, however, always had great respect for the integrity of her husband and saw him as God's chief messenger to her. She often said, "Not only is Milton my husband, he is also my pastor; I am the product of his ministry!" When Milton preached, she listened to what God was speaking into her life through her husband. She would review with him some of the key points that blessed her in the message he had given. She was also a great comfort to him, especially when he was emotionally drained.

For those who have never had a public ministry, it is difficult to know, or even imagine, the attacks the enemy of our souls directs against God's servants. Milton preached twice each Sunday for most of his life, and often preached or led a mid-week service. He poured himself emotionally, physically, and spiritually into these messages. When Monday morning rolled around, he was exhausted and often vulnerable to the devil's attack. The accusations came, bringing with them doubts about his effectiveness, emphasis on his failures, and whispers of worthlessness. Ruth learned to speak words of encouragement and comfort to Milton. She shared his burdens and prayed with her husband and, in the quietness of her personal devotions, prayed for him. They both grew. Milton developed great discipline and control over his emotional life. God gave Ruth a ministry to the wives of pastors. She knew their cares, burdens and trials. When she spoke at conferences, women were completely absorbed in her godly teaching.

Wherever Milton and Ruth ministered, God produced results. This was especially true in the last four churches they pastored: Martinez, California; Lewiston, Idaho; Ventura, California; and Eugene, Oregon. In each of these churches, God generated an awakening characterized by five distinct features: a harvest of lost people won to Christ; numbers of young people called into lives of service; gifts of the Holy Spirit and the miraculous evident; the baptism of the Holy Spirit received by many; and a pervasive sense of the presence of God, leading to holy living.

On several occasions in Martinez, prayer meetings would last most of the night. Children would have fallen asleep on the floor or in a pew while their parents prayed. As the light of a new day began to dawn, parents gathered them up and headed for home, perhaps weary in body, but refreshed in spirit and heart. It was not an overnight event, but a meeting with God that changed many permanently. Whole families were transformed by the move of the Holy Spirit. This transformation was evident over several generations, spanning more than half a century.

Since your author lived through many of Stewart's Lewiston years, allow me to summarize God's working in those two churches he pastored there. We all saw a day-by-day example of what it meant to live wholeheartedly for Christ, in Milton and Ruth. Not only did God work through them, but because they loved every person so fervently, we were drawn to the Lord. They saw us as important individuals who had unlimited potential in the hands of God; we saw in them the winsome beauty of our Lord.

When God begins to work through a congregation, it is a personal thing. Each person acts and reacts differently to what God desires to do in his life. During our prayer times, Milton was extremely sensitive to the needs of those praying. But he knew it was God Himself who would do His sovereign work in each open heart. Like a gentle shepherd caring for his flock, Milton moved among those praying, looking for opportunities to encourage, counsel, or simply agree in prayer with someone. Just as his preaching was effective in the building up of the whole body of Christ, so his ministry at the altar impacted us individually.

Isaiah had a vision of God (Isaiah 6) and was touched by a live coal from the altar. Isaiah's experience with God changed him and thrust him into his life's work. Even so, once an individual comes into the very presence of God, he cannot be the same, nor can he deny His reality. Believers certainly continue living in this world and all the good and bad of it, but in a very new way, they recognize their real citizenship is in heaven, with our splendid Lord.

It is a mystery how some people can be a part of a congregation where an awakening of God is occurring and be oblivious to it. A good scriptural example is in Jesus' parable of the sower and the seed. There were many kinds of ground upon which the seed fell. Each seed was the Word of God, but it fell into very different hearts. How important it is to keep our hearts open as freshly plowed ground, ready for the implantation of God's seed!

To those of us who were a part of their ministry, it seemed the Stewarts continually walked in the Spirit of God. The services were rarely predictable. From the opening prayer to the closing, the Lord orchestrated the meetings through Milton, His director. The elements of our time together usually contained singing, prayer and worship, the usual announcements, an offering, and preaching of the Word. We often got two or three bite-sized messages prior to the main sermon. But there were also special times when God enveloped us with His presence and the entire service was spent in prayer and worship. A lesser man could have made this special move of God a trumped-up event, but Milton's authenticity kept things in perspective. Everything was done according to the spirit and intent of Scripture.

Most of the sermons Milton preached had been prepared that week in his study. There were times when he walked into the pulpit with two sets of notes, stating, "I am not sure which of these sermons the Lord wants me to preach this morning. Which ever one it is not, you are likely to get it tonight...or next Sunday!" We bowed for prayer before he began his sermon, then one set of notes was chosen, and he started preaching. Some of us were always a little disappointed he didn't give us his titles and allow the congregation to vote!

But there were other times God was doing a divine work in people and the regular order of things was out the window. We had our youth service the hour before evening meeting started. Several times, God worked so effectively in the youth, their reaching out to the Lord would spill over into the evening service. Young people are so genuine, often a powerful example to the adults.

When the Stewarts moved to Ventura, California, God continued to manifest His power and grace through their ministry. One cannot put God in a box; it is futile to attempt to predict how His Holy Spirit will work. We are assured from Scripture of His love and care for His own, but how that happens cannot be predicted. He wants us to completely lean on Him for guidance. The board of Peoples Church was discussing the possibility of inviting a world-renowned evangelist to have meetings with them. This man was willing to come, and the men were excited at the possibility. As this continued to be discussed among them, the Lord spoke clearly to Milton that having this man was not the will of God.

When he told his men, "I am not going to extend an invitation for this man to come," they were disappointed, but accepted his decision reluctantly. One of the men was quite offended by Milton's decision, and spoke strongly against him. Several weeks later, this board member, as a part of his work responsibility as a juvenile social service worker, was called upon to investigate suspicious behavior in a parked car. When he arrived, he found this evangelist in the backseat of the automobile in a compromising relationship with a teenaged boy. At the next board meeting, much to his credit, this man stood in front of his peers and apologized for his mistrust of his pastor's leadership. "You saved the reputation of this church and our families untold damage by listening to the voice of the Lord. Thank you, Pastor Stewart."

There are many "voices" we hear in our inner man, but Milton learned to distinguish the Lord's voice from all others. Early in his ministry in Ventura, he went up on a hill where a cross stood overlooking the city. He began praying over the town, asking God for His blessings and the manifestation of His power in that area through the Holy Spirit. While he was standing there, the Lord spoke to him. "You have a lot to do and only three years to do it!" When God began stirring his heart three years later, the clarity of God's message on the hill was a positive reminder to follow His leading.

At Eugene's Lighthouse Temple, the Stewarts met on Wednesday evenings in the lower youth auditorium for special services. There was teaching, prayer, and openness to the moving of the Holy Spirit, which was not practical in the Sunday morning or evening services. It was designed for people who knew the Lord, not outsiders. Its focus was to simply worship and draw near the Lord. Freedom was available to exercise spiritual gifts of prophecy, tongues and interpretation of tongues, healing, words of knowledge and wisdom. God's Spirit did amazing things among the people. Milton often stated how beautiful it was to be on the platform watching God work among His people. He often felt completely detached from what was going on in front of him, like a spectator observing the Master at work. He certainly was not "working his audience" to project a preconceived outcome. The miraculous and supernatural happened, and God was the Author of it all.

Following a Wednesday evening meeting, Milton was standing by the hall door when he was approached by a schoolteacher. This lady had such poor eyesight she wore both glasses and contacts simultaneously. Milton offered prayer for her before she left. In the morning, as was her habit, she put in her contact lenses, but they blurred badly. Grabbing her glasses from the bedside table, she adjusted them carefully on her face, opened her eyes and couldn't see anything at all. Removing both glasses and contacts cleared up everything. God had healed her eyes! Her optometrist gave her a thorough exam and declared she now had 20/20 vision.

While Milton was regional superintendent, he accepted an invitation to preach at an Open Bible church in Dayton, Ohio. As he was leading the congregation in worship, the Lord gave him a word of prophecy to speak to the people. Upon hearing the prophecy, it was as though the breath of God blew upon the audience and they all fell to the floor under the power of God. Great worship broke out as God's presence moved among individuals. Milton was startled. He couldn't recall a word of the prophecy he had spoken under the inspiration of the Spirit, but the results were the sovereign work of God. God had taken the service out of Milton's hands and done His will among His people. Milton liked orderly services, but when God's Spirit moved, he had no complaints about the outcome.

The preaching and ministry of Milton Stewart was a direct fulfillment of the great commission given by our Lord. In describing the ministry of the apostles, Mark says, "Then the disciples went out and preached everywhere, and the Lord worked with them and confirmed his word by the signs that accompanied it" (Mark 16:20). Should this not be the norm for our ministers and churches today?

* * *

Chapter Thirteen

Shepherding the Pastors

*"For this reason I remind you to fan into
flame the gift of God, which is in you
through the laying on of my hands."*
2 Timothy 1:6

Even when God gives you the desire of your
heart, it can come as a shock. When the Pacific
Division of Open Bible Churches held their 1969
fall convention, Milton had no premonition his name
would be placed into nomination for the office of
superintendent, but it was. He was happy to be pastor
of Lighthouse Temple and had no plans to leave. Two
people he had a good deal of respect for, however,
urged him to withdraw his name. He went to the Lord
with his quandary. Standing alone that evening in the
parking lot between the church and the Bible school,
he cried out to God for an answer. "Lord," he prayed,

"I need assurance from You whether or not this is the right thing for me to do."

Milton was a preacher, not a business administrator. To oversee the affairs of this large region was, according to his résumé, not within his qualifications. His main motivation in even allowing his name to be considered was to come alongside the pastors as an encourager and helper, and that was hardly a part of the job description. In the face of many self-doubts, he asked God for guidance. He was not expecting the answer he received from the Lord, but it brought great peace to his heart. "Milton," the Spirit of the Lord said, "whatever you decide to do, I'll be with you!" That settled it. He ran and was elected by the regional pastors.

Milton had barely moved into his office in downtown Eugene when he faced the first crisis. The Southern California district superintendent called, telling him to come down for an ugly problem in one of the churches. This body of believers was affiliated with Open Bible Churches, but the pastor rarely attended district meetings or cooperated with other area churches. They had steadily lost their congregation, which was down to sixteen people, all but one of whom were members of the pastor's extended family. When Milton arrived at the church, the meeting had already begun. The pastor announced there would be only two items of business. It was obviously a well-coached gathering.

One of the relatives stood and moved that the church withdraw its membership from Open Bible

Churches. This was seconded. Another relative stood, moving that the church and its assets be placed for sale. This also was seconded.

Milton then rose, pronouncing, "I see this is a well-planned meeting, but I have a right to speak. This congregation is affiliated with Open Bible Churches, and based upon that affiliation, I vote against both these motions. This business has been planned without the knowledge of the regional office, and that is not right."

Ignoring Milton's words, the pastor called for the vote. Both measures passed, with Milton dissenting. The pastor placed the property on the market, then, following the sale, pocketed the proceeds. Milton vowed never to allow that to happen again on his watch. But he also had a talk with the Lord about his new job. If this incident were any example of the work God expected him to be doing, he would just as soon resign now and go back to pastoring. As shocked as he was by his first official regional business, he knew the promise of the Word, "Never will I leave you; never will I forsake you" (Hebrews 13:5). And there had been that special word from the Lord in the parking lot of the church. He made his choice, absolutely believing God would be with him.

Several years later, another pastor attempted to disengage his congregation from Open Bible. Although all Open Bible churches were owned by the local congregations, they could not be sold or transferred without proper notification and a congregational vote at an officially called meeting. At this church's official meeting, Milton stood and declared to the pastor, "By the authority vested in me by the Pacific Regional Board of Open Bible, I hereby declare your credentials in Open Bible Churches to be revoked. You are no longer the pastor of this church or a member of Open Bible Churches." The pastor was livid, but Milton's board had given him authority for this action. The Pacific region sold the church properties, placing the proceeds in a special capital funds account.

Milton's predecessor in the office, Harvey Klapstein, had begun a systematic search for all church properties formerly listed with Open Bible's Pacific region. Milton continued checking these, as well as updating the legal documents of existing churches. While in office, he found properties long-since forgotten and abandoned that had belonged to past Open Bible congregations. Liquidating these church assets eventually allowed the region to construct its own office building debt-free.

Harvey Klapstein, former college president and regional superintendent, along with current college president, Ed Wood, gave great energy to raising money for the new campus buildings at Eugene Bible College. To fund construction, they hired a financial planner who sold bonds to members of Open Bible Churches' congregations throughout the Pacific region. These bonds' maturity dates obligated the school to pay them off at maturation. Interest rates across the nation were beginning to rise, and our country was caught in a severe money crunch.

Milton saw this matter as an immediate need to be addressed. He came to several conclusions:

- He did not have the financial expertise or desire to continue selling bonds for the school's building program.
- It was too costly to hire a professional fundraiser.
- Due to the nationwide economic downturn, he could foresee problems the school may have in repaying the bonds when they came due.
- He believed those who bought the bonds did so because they believed in Eugene Bible College and its future.
- He was willing to personally ask each investor if they would prayerfully consider giving the amount of money invested in bonds to EBC as a gift.

After presenting his conclusions and plans to the regional board, he was given the go-ahead. He preached to a congregation on Sunday, and stayed over Monday to have one-on-one talks with those who had purchased bonds. It took more than a year to complete all contacts with churches in Washington, Idaho, Oregon, and California, but the results were astounding. One hundred percent of those holding bonds agreed to give them as a gift to Eugene Bible College.

Milton's vision for his region had one consolidating goal—evangelism. His plan, adjusted from the World Evangelism program of the national office, would be communicated to the region's churches over three nights. The two major burdens on Milton's heart were world evangelization and the development of the EBC campus for training workers. With Eugene Bible College and world missions on the front burners, Milton sold the program to the region's pastors, then, ordering World Evangelism materials from the national office, scheduled meetings and secured missionary speakers. One night was given to each of three areas. Milton, the keynote speaker, preached on the home vision, Don Bryan, newly-appointed EBC president, spoke on Eugene Bible College, and a visiting missionary presented the foreign mission challenge on the final night. Congregations were encouraged to make faith promises, payable over the coming year. As the promises were received, the income was divided according to an agreed-upon percentage.

The success of World Evangelism conferences was unprecedented. Pastors and churches were convinced of the program's success, and for several years Milton and Don were on the road hosting similar conferences, their school van loaded with World Evangelism materials. There was usually an intense two-month period when they were continually away from home, followed by three or four months of three-day conferences. The results were rewarding, but it was a grinding schedule.

Ruth Stewart knew how much Milton needed her at his side, but it was difficult even to contemplate leaving their teenaged son John behind while both parents traveled. Thank God for Don and Ruth Bryan! They understood the dilemma their friends were in and were willing to help. During the weeks Ruth Stewart was on the road, John stayed with the Bryan family. For John, it may not have been home, but he got along well with the three younger Bryan children, and the situation was ameliorated. Few people could have handled this multi-tasking better than Ruth Stewart. Because of the challenging schedule, she had a practical glimpse into the great sacrifice her missionary friends made when they had to be absent from their children while doing the Lord's work.

David had his Jonathan, and Milton Stewart had his Don Bryan. The two men could not have been more different in personality, gifting, and style, yet they became fast friends on a number of levels. For the cause of World Evangelism to be advanced through the Pacific region churches, the two men traveled untold thousands of miles by van, speaking, raising money, and promoting the causes of the Bible college, missions and other programs of Open Bible Churches.

Don was a detail man. He could give all the facts needed to know about anything for which he carried the responsibility. No one could outwork him. He was dogged and determined, fixed on the goals before him. Encompassing all these characteristics was a heart for God's work and a great desire to bring glory to God's kingdom. It was this like-mindedness with Milton that cemented their relationship.

Because Don was a part of the Pacific Region Board, Milton leaned on him for administrative help. When issues or people needed to be confronted, Don was willing to help. Likewise, Milton was happy to come to Don's side when the school was facing difficulties. The school's budget was more subject to ups and downs than the regional office, so Milton, with his board's approval, was always ready to assist when the school's cash flow was low and bills were due.

Both men, at different times, owned Ford Mustangs; Don also had a Ford Thunderbird he was renovating. When they were out on the road, it was hard not to turn in at an auto wrecking yard in search of parts. One Sunday morning, the two men were dressed for a church service in Klamath Falls, Oregon. They were quite a bit early, so when Don spotted a wrecking yard, he pulled in. As they walked among the discarded cars, Don discovered a Ford Thunderbird, exactly the year of his—and those special tail lights looked in perfect condition. He got the owner to open the trunk, then borrowing the needed tools, he crawled in and removed that beautiful set of tail lights.

Milton has forever etched in his brain a picture of his friend, dressed to the nines in dark suit, tie, and starched shirt, sitting cross-legged in the trunk of that dusty old car on a Sunday morning, unscrewing a set of lights for his T-bird back home. Don got those lights, dusted himself off, and the two men arrived at church no worse for the junkyard stopover.

Family time was also a shared experience between the two households. Not only was John welcome at the Bryans when his parents were on the road, but often the families enjoyed holidays and weekend meals together. Ruth Bryan and Ruth Stewart were partners in ministry, just like their husbands. Both women were well-balanced leaders, mature in their faith, influential in their own rights, and strongly supportive of their husbands. Having mutual friends of such caliber was a God-given gift both families cherished for over twenty years in Eugene and throughout their lives.

Milton knew from his own early ministerial experience how valuable a word of encouragement to a young pastor could be. His goal of visiting all 80+ churches in his region was accomplished during his first few years, and in that time, Milton got to know the pastors, their spouses, their children, and even most of their pets. When Milton was staying with the Jim Pluimer family in Martinez, he became acquainted with Jocko, their little dog. On one visit, three young children, Kristi, Kim, and Kevin, were crying because Jocko was deathly sick. Milton, ever sensitive to the hearts of children, prayed for the dog, and God healed it.

Mentoring his pastors was never a formalized plan with Milton. They knew he was interested in them, cared about their families and their work in the church, and that as a man of God, he would stand with them, praying and helping in any way possible. They would never be left without a person who deeply cared about them personally. As he met the children of pastors, he connected with them, remembering their names, asking about them and closely following their lives. Milton continually opened himself to these families, making himself available to counsel, pray, or encourage them as the Spirit of God led him.

Young pastors were of special concern to Milton; they could easily become discouraged when difficulties arose. He saw to it that discretionary money was available in the regional accounts to help fill needs. Seeing David and Julie Cole work so hard in their Southern California church while David was enrolled at Fuller Seminary touched Milton's heart. David carried the stress of his church in addition to his doctoral program, while Julie cared for their new baby. They existed on meager resources. Milton found some extra funds with which he paid their hospital bill.

Many pastors, at one time or another, received help through the regional office. Milton's integrity and connection with his pastors engendered a great spirit of trust regarding the region's funds and Milton's use of those funds during his years in office. In his eyes, people were more important than programs or plans. When pastor Ken Brown would drop by the regional office, he might ask, "Milton, do you have just a minute?" His ready response: "Ken, I always will have time for you!" Dropping whatever he was doing, Milton absorbed himself in the person who had called on him. His secretary, Marilyn Brown, never saw him turn anyone away because he was too busy. He may have had to take his work home, but people came first. Every person and circumstance was different, but people were made to feel important, and Milton's heart was bound to them in love. Illustrations of his connections with men and women are abundant. A few are recorded in the "Tributes" chapter at the end of this book.

At this point, however, I want to focus on one man's experiences under Milton Stewart's leadership, and the transforming influence it had upon his life. Bob Laflin's testimony can be multiplied many times over in the lives of men and women the Stewarts loved so dearly.

Bob Laflin was born in Cincinnati, Ohio, raised a Catholic, and joined the Air Force during the Vietnam War. While stationed in Alaska, a friend talked to him about a personal relationship with Jesus Christ, and encouraged him, when he got saved, to "Tell somebody about it and then find a Bible-preaching church." In 1974, he was living at McChord Air Force Base near Tacoma, Washington. At 10:00 p.m., on January 12, while alone in the barracks, the Spirit of God spoke to Bob. He immediately gave his heart to Christ and began looking for a good Bible church. Visiting McKinley Hill Open Bible Church of Tacoma, he found a great body of believers led by pastor Ron Swanson. After two years, he became a part-time student at EBC, then enrolled full time in the winter of 1978 to study for the ministry.

Milton Stewart was regional superintendent at the time, often speaking at the EBC chapels. He could see God had His hand on Bob's life, and encouraged him in his faith. When he graduated from EBC, Bob was especially blessed when Milton prayed over him, dedicating him to the Lord's service. Following graduation, Bob moved back to Tacoma to work as an associate pastor at McKinley Hill for two and a half years, then spent a year at the Centralia Open Bible Church where he was given a chance to preach more often. God was building into his ministry both evangelistic and prophetic gifts. A five-day revival meeting he held in Centralia was visited by an unusual move of the Spirit of God. This was a confirming sign to Bob of God's leading and calling in his life.

When he returned to Eugene in the mid-1980s, Bob attended Lighthouse Temple with Pastor Bill Johnson, immediately holding evangelistic meetings wherever God opened doors for him. He had the full backing and recommendation of Milton Stewart and Pastor Johnson. When not busy with meetings, he served the Bible college as an adjunct teacher. The following year, Milton invited him to come to his office and help organize his library.

Working in the regional office while Milton was present became a most positive experience. While Bob dug through Milton's personal library, he was privileged to observe Milton carry out the daily business of the region. And what an honor to have access to Milton's wealth of books! Bob was surprised at the evident wear displayed on many of them, a witness to heavy use. As he organized and cataloged these books, he was impressed with their quality, diversity, and depth of subject matter. The sections on the Holy Spirit and the Pentecostal movement were especially comprehensive.

It came to Bob's attention that Milton's secretary, Marilyn Brown, capably handled much of the administrative work, leaving Milton more freedom for his concerns for the ministers in his region. His genuine welcome to drop-in visitors was an indication of his accessibility. It was apparent that these pastors, and other visitors, regarded Milton as a man of integrity, a friend, and a solid source of advice.

Bob also thought very highly of EBC President Don Bryan, recognizing in him a different set of gifts. Don was an experienced administrator and a tough detail man. Give him the ball, show him the goal, and get out of his way. Milton was ever the visionary, with dreams, ambitions, and prophetic words for his men. Bob was strongly influenced by both these leaders, realizing how God used their strengths within Open Bible Churches to complement each other.

During times when they could interact personally, Milton shared with Bob his convictions on giving, on believing God's Word, and trusting God's call on his life. He unabashedly would look him in the eye and tell him that he loved him and believed God's hand was upon him for great ministry. Bob was always reassured that Milton was praying for him. Milton recognized him as unique, with a calling in ministry unlike most men. Although he did not have a specific sense of direction for Bob, or how he might be fully used within Open Bible Churches, he validated God's call on his life through prayer and encouragement.

Bob took the following notes on a sermon Milton preached May 15, 1980, a few days before Bob graduated from EBC.

"To Be Used of God"

Do you like being used of God? Who enjoys being used by Him?

Mark 16:20 "Then the disciples went out and preached everywhere, and the Lord worked with them..."

Second Corinthians 6:1 (KJV) "We then, as workers together with him..."

God is not looking to use us, but to work with us.

Illustration: Like a yoke of oxen, we are yoked together with Christ in life and ministry. This yoke was made to fit us. As Jesus said, "For my yoke is easy and my burden is light" (Matthew 11:30)! As long as you keep going and don't balk, the yoke will make no scars on your neck.

People use people for their own ends. The devil uses people for his ends.

God doesn't use us. He works with us.

As we live in union with Him, God honors the decisions we make and works them out for His glory.

It is as though God says, "You furnish the ideas; I'll furnish the power!"

We are "workers together with him."

There were phrases Milton used in his preaching that stuck in Bob's mind—phrases like "Trust your anointing;" "The enabling comes with the doing;" "The church is asleep, and can't wake itself up!" Milton had a marvelous way of communicating, using words and phrases which seemed to have mental glue all over them. Wherever the Stewarts ministered, people remembered his inimitable messages.

Bob summed up his relationship with Milton: "For thirty years, he has been my friend, encourager and mentor. He has prayed and prophesied over me and been instrumental in launching my personal ministry. Milton is a prayer warrior, a person of integrity, generous to a fault, a unique individual. He is in love with Jesus Christ, his wife, Ruth, and their family. He loves God's Word and all humanity, especially ministers of the Gospel. God has given him great wisdom. He has been faithful to God's call and to the body of Christ through his chosen denomination, Open Bible Churches. I will ever be grateful for his personal interest and the impact his life has had on mine."

When Milton became regional superintendent of the Pacific region, he was privileged, through this office, also to be a member of the national board of Open Bible Churches. He served for twenty-two years in this capacity under general superintendents Ray Smith and Frank W. Smith. This board was made up of the general superintendent, all regional superintendents, the director of missions, and the secretary/treasurer.

Several years into his job as regional superintendent, this national board sought long-range direction for its organization. There was some ambivalence regarding the organization's function in the body of Christ. Other denominations having similar doctrines and practices had become dominant in the charismatic movement. Should Open Bible Churches merge with another body, or carry on as an independent entity? A meeting was scheduled in Branson, Missouri, with another larger denomination, to discuss amalgamation. When Milton left the meeting, as discussed in the "Preaching" chapter, he was quite distraught. As he prayed and asked God for answers, not just for himself, but for his denomination, the Lord spoke to his heart.

There are several things that need to be said before we go on. Milton never asked God to give him the gift of prophecy. It came as a gift to him out of the intimacy and obedience in his relationship with Christ. No prophet in the Bible had an easy time. As with Milton, they were misunderstood, misinterpreted, and sometimes outright persecuted, even by those closest to them. But God does not withdraw his gifts, and Milton bore with great grace this difficult calling from God.

It is impossible to analyze how God speaks to someone. He is continually speaking to us, but through some people God gives special words or prophetic utterances. These came to Milton in a variety of ways. Many times when he gave a prophecy, he would forget it almost immediately. On other occasions, if the prophecy was spoken to him and for a personal situation, the words of the Lord were seared into his being. He couldn't forget them if he wanted to.

"Lord, what is the place of Open Bible Churches in the plan of God?" As he flew home, this question to God burrowed deeply into his heart. When the Lord spoke to Milton regarding the question, each word attached itself to his heart and mind. "Open Bible Churches serves a vital function in the body of Christ, and has a divine destiny." He began asking God questions, and in his spirit, carried on a conversation with the Lord. "What does 'vital function' mean?" The answer came in an illustration, "Would you lose a 'vital function' if you were to lose a hand? An arm? A leg? An eye? The answer is NO, because you have two hands, arms, legs and eyes. But if you were to lose your heart or brain or liver, you would lose a vital part, because you couldn't function without it."

At the next convening of the Pacific Regional Board, following the National Board's discussion of amalgamation in Branson, Milton shared a report of the meeting, and concluded with his new vision of the place of Open Bible Churches in the plan of God. What a thrilling session!

He began to share this message with the pastors in his region. Most were eager to hear, and were encouraged in the Lord. When one pastor seriously questioned him about it, he refused to argue, simply saying, "I only know what God told me." Milton carried this message and the vow to speak only what was in the Word, or what God had told him, through the remainder of his ministry. This message was preached in most of the Pacific region churches, and numerous other churches to which he was invited. In R. Bryant Mitchell's book, *Heritage and Horizons*, a book chronicling the history of Open Bible Churches,

Milton speaks on p. 380 of this vision God gave him for his denomination:

> I believe that we have a divine destiny, which God has given to us...We are not an accident or the extension of some man's ego. God Almighty moved on our forefathers. Our movement is man-made, but divinely ordained...We have a ministry to perform... I am not afraid of institutionalism. It speaks to me of strength, security, and stability... The enemy would like to fragment us, but we will not allow this... I believe that Open Bible Standard serves a vital function in the body of Christ... I feel that we have swung so far to the teaching type of ministry that we do not have prophets any more. We need prophets. We must listen to the voice of our own prophets. A prophet produces prophets... I feel that out of us are to come men and women who not only teach, but who declare and proclaim... Can one man change an organization? One man can change the world.

In 1978, Milton contributed a series of articles to the "Message," the official publication of OBC. Titling the series "Divine Dynamics," he introduced the topic by paraphrasing the words of Jesus at His ascension: "You are to continue and complete what I have begun, but you will never do it on the natural level. I promise you an enabler, a revealer, an empowerer, who will, through you, defeat the enemy and establish the church and win the lost."

These written messages were a blessing to pastors throughout the organization, challenging and awakening men and women to the realities of our partnership with Christ in the dissemination of the Gospel.

Not preaching every Sunday was an awkward adjustment for Milton. Instead, he found himself on Sundays listening to one of his pastors preach. But when he was invited to speak, it was a delight, and he thoroughly prepared himself for that special occasion. Many of the sermons he preached within the Pacific region were a part of World Evangelism Conferences or other prescribed events. He had no problems finding excellent biblical material to fit the occasion. The one to feel sorry for was his traveling companion, Don Bryan, who may have been listening to the message for the fortieth time.

Many sermons were favorites, but he sensitively opened his mind and heart to the leading of the Holy Spirit in his choice of the message. Before all else, what did God wish to say through him to this particular congregation? Ruth remembers a number of times she watched God speak to her husband as he walked from his chair to the platform. The Lord would drop an entire message, complete with illustrations, into his heart in a moment's time. She said it was like electricity from heaven. This was a fresh *rhema* directly from the heart of God.

After the Lord spoke so distinctly to him about the future of OBC, Milton often encouraged his audiences with variations of that message. What marked his sermons, setting them apart from the ordinary, was the anointing of the Holy Spirit. He spoke with great conviction. He knew the Scriptures and believed them with every fiber of his being. He was unafraid to tackle some of the most incredible verses including:

"…anyone who has faith in me will do what I have been doing. He will do even greater things than these, because I am going to the Father" (John 14:12).

"I have given them the glory that you gave me, that they may be one as we are one. I in them and you in me…" (John 16:22-23).

"For in Christ all the fullness of the Deity lives in bodily form, and you have been given fullness in Christ, who is the head over every power and authority" (Colossians 2:9-10).

Milton challenged his congregations to believe the Word of God, even when it flew in the face of natural reasoning. He had a sermon titled, "Facts, Figures, and Faith in God." Illustrating profusely through Old Testament miracles, he boldly proclaimed our faith in Almighty God is superior to, and more powerful than, anything the devil can throw at us.

A church member from southern Oregon, who occasionally was privileged to hear Milton preach, commented, "He usually didn't get through his introduction, but there was more meat in it than in a dozen regular sermons."

Wherever Milton and Ruth preached the Gospel, an indelible imprint was made on the lives of people. They may have carried a visual memory of the messenger, but the Holy Spirit engrafted the Word of God in people's hearts as he spoke. God used him as a channel for His voice to the congregation. Milton often said, "Truth is too big to be contained in a 30-minute sermon. It sparkles in so many dimensions. It takes a lifetime to begin getting your heart, mind, and faith around the truths of God's precious Word."

Ken Brown, who has known Milton from the time Ken pastored his first church until his retirement, remarked, "Milton Stewart doesn't have a political bone in his body." Although Milton worked hard at pastoring and was diligent in the business affairs of his office as regional superintendent, he never promoted himself for a higher office.

In 1976, Ray Smith resigned as general superintendent of OBC to take the pastorate at Lighthouse Temple in Eugene. Frank W. Smith, who had served as assistant superintendent with Ray, was elected general superintendent. In 1977, Milton was chosen by the delegates to fill the unoccupied seat of assistant superintendent of OBC. He served in that capacity for fourteen years before retiring in 1991.

* * *

Chapter Fourteen

Finishing the Course

"I press on toward the goal to win the prize
for which God has called me
heavenward in Christ Jesus."
Philippians 3:14

Since its inception, the regional office had been located in rented office spaces in Eugene, Oregon. As the new EBC campus sprouted, Milton recognized how valuable it would be to have the regional office on those same grounds. He bargained for two acres of property on the campus site in exchange for the division's share of a real estate asset owned jointly by school and regional office. The board approved his plan, clearing up two problems with the transfer.

They hired Mr. Washburn, the architect who had designed and built the new Lighthouse Temple. Since the land was sloping, it was relatively easy to include a daylight basement at minimal extra cost. Milton's initial plans called for a good-sized superintendent's office with bathroom, an office for the director of Women's World Fellowship, and a conference room with kitchenette for board meetings. The secretary/receptionist's office was part of the open entry. A file-storage room, bathrooms, and closets completed the top level. The lower level included two large rooms with restrooms and necessary amenities. Following the completion of the building, several EBC students roomed in the basement while their new dormitory was being completed. Dan MacIntyre, from the Lighthouse Temple congregation, was chosen by the board to construct the building.

Ken Brown may very well have had a talk with Dan, warning him that Milton might want to strap on a tool belt and help with the construction. When Ken accompanied Milton to Powers, Oregon, to close that church, Milton told him of his carpentry fiasco there. One weekend, Milton decided to rebuild the church's main entrance porch. Working all day and into the night, he finally completed it around midnight. Waking Ruth to show her the new porch, they walked through the church to the front door, which they found jammed shut. He had built the porch too high and the door couldn't open. Milton sawed enough off the supports to allow the front door to swing free. By 1:00 a.m. everything was back in place.

Thankfully, Milton was too busy to even consider strapping on his tool belt for Dan MacIntyre. When Dan and his crew finished the building in 1979, a dedication service was held to thank God. The regional office was debt-free, paid for completely by money from the sale of surplus OBC properties. Ruth was especially tickled to have her own WWF office. The students got a continual view of the project, since the structure was situated on a lower corner of the EBC campus. The roofline reminded many of a Pizza Hut fast food outlet. Lots of good-natured teasing ensued.

With the regional office now functioning, Milton's attention turned toward another project. What construction did God want to do in the men of his region? What aspirations, dreams and hopes did he have for his pastors? The writings of Peter, Paul, John, and Luke were full of admonitions. But it was the empowering presence of the Holy Spirit making the dominating difference in New Testament ministry. He longed for his men to hunger for such experience.

His own ministry was jump-started through the baptism in the Holy Spirit. His first five years of preaching had been without the empowering of the Holy Spirit. When that took place in Martinez, California, it opened his whole life to what a "visitation from God" meant. The very next Sunday he opened the pulpit Bible, and God simply took over, speaking through him. A great visitation from the Lord lasting twelve days saturated the church. It was God doing His thing, not the invention of any person or program. Because of these experiences, Milton was not functioning in a pretense of super-spirituality, but with a great desire that every minister of the

Gospel possess that same expectation of the working of the Holy Spirit.

As he visited Open Bible Churches, he began sharing what he had personally seen God do. Since God did not play favorites, He would do the same for anybody. His driving motivation became to encourage ministers to believe God would do in their lives what He had done for Milton. A great revival of the Holy Spirit is going on now in many Latin American countries and throughout Africa. Why? Those people, in their simplicity, are taking God's Word literally, and are seeing people saved, healed, and delivered. God is validating their faith through His mighty power.

After becoming regional superintendent, Milton and Ruth had lunch with an interesting couple. These people had flown all over the country, investigating revivals, special moves of the Lord, or any religious happening they felt was genuine. They did not want to miss out on anything God might be doing. After the meal, this couple and Ruth went on outside while Milton paid the tab. As he stood waiting to pay the bill, the Lord spoke clearly to his heart. "Whatever I am going to do in my Kingdom, you'll be the first to know." The message frightened him! He was astounded!

Later, he began to read what Jesus said to his disciples. In Luke 17:20-25, they were told not to run after every report of a visitation of the Son of Man. Since the Kingdom was within them, they would "be the first to know." And John 15:14-15 stated, "You are my friends if you do what I command. I no longer call you servants, because a servant does not know his master's business. Instead, I have called you friends, for everything that I learned from my Father I have made known to you." The message, "You'll be the first to know" was not exclusive, but what Jesus promised to share with all His friends. The body of Christ is not going to be splintered into thousands of factions by visitations of God in various places around the world, but it will be "Built up until we all reach unity in the faith and in the knowledge of the Son of God and become mature, attaining to the whole measure of the fullness of Christ" (Ephesians 4:12-13).

This Holy Spirit-driven message would be shared three ways:

1. Milton needed to be an example of what it meant to walk in the fullness of the Holy Spirit.
2. The revealed Word of God was foundational. If ministers believed and acted upon the Word, God would validate their ministry. Hebrews 2:4
3. He would love and pray for each of his men, accepting them as individuals with differing gifts, and affirming them in their ministry.

Many testify to the warmth of welcome they always received when meeting Milton and Ruth. They both engaged people personally, learning their names and remembering faces. You felt within their inner circle from the first time you met them.

This genuine spirit endeared them to the people they were called to serve. There would always be people who resisted their graciousness, wishing to keep Stewarts at arms length, but that was hard to do. Stewarts would pray for you. And when you got into their prayer life, the barriers usually came tumbling down.

This same friendliness was on display at the regional office. First impressions there are usually borne by the secretary/receptionist, and Milton worked with four fine ladies during his 18 years in office: Lila, Julie Quezada, Joy Haines, and finally Marilyn Brown. Marilyn and her husband, Norm, had servant hearts. As receptionist, she cultivated an atmosphere of acceptance. Her husband was such a handyman, Milton often said, "I got two for the price of one when I hired Marilyn!" She volunteered Norm for all kinds of things needing to be done by saying, "Oh, Norm will take care of that!" And he did. He could fix nearly anything.

Marilyn Brown functioned as office manager for Milton, but like all previous secretaries, she handled all of the money for the organization. When special offerings at conferences were taken, she enlisted help counting and recording funds. Normally, she alone was responsible for writing receipts, depositing money, and paying bills with checks signed by her boss. Most importantly, she kept the financial ledgers for the region.

Marilyn was very concerned when Milton told her of a confidentiality leak. He reviewed the matter with her, and they agreed it looked as though the information must have been disseminated from their office. Marilyn gulped. She *was* the office. Milton was never accusatory toward her, but she certainly felt on the spot. After digging out both the source and truth of the leak, she happily informed Milton of her discovery. Confidentiality was paramount when working with the ministers of the region. Any person working with Milton certainly knew that "loose lips sink ships," and he expected the business of the division's ministry to stay within the office.

It did not take Marilyn long to notice that her boss was a generous giver. When Milton took a church offering for a regional need, he also gave toward that cause. When given an honorarium for speaking at a church, he felt it should go directly to the regional office, since he was an employee of OBC.

Quite often when he was on the road visiting churches, he saw a definite need in a minister's life, and a gift would be given to help. What many people did not know was that it often did not come from the regional office, but from Milton's travel-expense account, or from his personal finances.

Ruth could be just as generous. She and Jesse Wall, the Men of Vision leader, were always looking out for Marilyn. When a conference meeting was on the horizon, Marilyn attended. From their department funds, they would each contribute enough to purchase a new outfit for Marilyn. The Stewarts followed the scriptural admonition on giving, "…if it is contributing to the needs of others, let him give generously" (Romans 12:8).

The men of the Pacific region came to understand their business was being handled in an orderly and timely manner. Making ministerial background checks, issuing preaching credentials, and renewing documents were vital responsibilities demanding timeliness. Being efficient did not lessen the warmth shown to all. An enthusiastic reception let visitors to the office know they were welcome. Milton often took personal time to talk with visitors, reflecting his own convictions that people are of higher importance than programs and deskwork.

Twice a year the board of the Pacific region met for business sessions. Since the April ministers' conference gathered all licensed preachers of the region together at a given location, the board scheduled one meeting at that time. The other meeting would be booked at a different location in the fall. Regional board members consisted of the six district superintendents, the president of Eugene Bible College, and Milton, as regional superintendent—eight in total. The district board members received no stipend for their work on the regional board, but were reimbursed for travel and meeting expenses. Several years after he had been elected to the regional office, Milton took a good look at the cost of these board meetings. Studying past conference expenses, he found a meeting in Hawaii would have a cost comparable to one held in a major west coast city. It would also be an enjoyable perk for his men, so he booked reservations in Honolulu.

The weather and laid-back atmosphere of the islands was a welcome change for the group. Business occupied most of the day, but Milton had scheduled a cultural activity for one of the evenings. At the hotel, a group of islanders would tell the story of their history through song, costume, dance, and narration. Now, one of the things you never had to question about Milton was his moral character. Not only has he always been a one-woman man, he would never knowingly allow any improprieties to seep into his life. He lived and conducted his ministry about as straight as anyone could. However, that evening during the program, Don Bryan leaned over and whispered in his ear, "I don't think you can see this, but I wanted you to know that those young ladies up there aren't wearing anything on top." With Milton's poor eyesight, all he had noticed was the waist-length hair of the island girls! Milton's men got a lot of mileage out of that incident in good-natured teasing of their boss.

By far, the toughest issue Milton and his board faced was the discipline of ministers who fell into moral failure. Because circumstances could be extremely different in each case, the men discussed individuals in light of God's Word, and recommended the next step to be taken. Some wished to be extremely firm, others wanted mercy to reign and still others straddled lines. There were no easy resolutions. When it was possible, Milton had a one-on-one meeting with the fallen minister, discussing the matter thoroughly with him. He was careful to let him know he would stand by his side through whatever discipline/restoration was recommended by the board. Milton tried to be consistent by keeping his eye on the final goal — restoration. He believed if such a fallen person repented, had an adequate amount of time away from ministry to heal, and had the love and support of his fellow ministers, he could be redeemed. The debates surrounding these discussions were difficult.

One such minister had been involved in moral failure years before. Through the discipline and eventual restoration of the man to his calling, Milton had been his friend and encourager. As he lay dying, this pastor asked his wife to call Milton. His wife shared with Milton her husband's great gratitude over the love and kind support he had given him through those dark days of recovery.

No meetings were ever launched without being seasoned with much prayer. The men shared needs of churches and pastors under their district care. Milton emphasized the necessity of confidentiality within their circle. He also jotted personal comments regarding the pastors or churches that were hurting. When he returned to his office, a thorough review of his notes would result in continued prayer and individual encouragement written to his family of pastors. Marilyn was often directed to make out a check from the regional office to accompany a note. He could always find extra funds within his budget to help a struggling minister through a difficult time. There was a strong, trusting relationship between the board and its superintendent, and when financial reports were under scrutiny, the use of funds to help ministers was not a concern.

There is nothing like the sweet fellowship of brothers united in accomplishing the work of the Kingdom. Milton's style of leadership gave the men complete freedom to express themselves. After introducing a topic on the agenda, Milton or one of the men closer to the matter, would give all the necessary background. Then the floor would open for discussion. He was conscious of staying evenhanded, not allowing one person to dominate the discussion unnecessarily. He treated everyone fairly and above board. Great respect was accorded him for this.

Sometimes your own friends will test your mettle. Milton wasn't expecting it, but when a couple of men opposed him on a plan he felt was important to the region, he thought the matter over. Milton decided they were not sincere in their dissention, but simply wished to test their superintendent. It was probably also apparent to others around the table, so Milton stepped up. "Gentlemen," he calmly announced, "when I was in college, I took enough boxing to know what to do when I was maneuvered into a corner. Now we are gathered here doing God's work, yet some of you would like nothing better than to see me backed against the ropes. Let me give you fair warning that you are going to end up in far worse shape than I when we emerge from the corner." The men were stunned for a moment, then the grins broke out and his board gave him a standing ovation.

When the work of the board was finished for the day, the men would enjoy leisure time together. It was good to relax, talk, and catch up on the families and activities of one another. Since these men knew each other well, practical jokes and a good measure of levity helped get the starch out of their systems. Occasionally the men would press Don Bryan into singing his famous, "Who Shot the Hole in My Sombrero?" Milton heard it often when Don grew tired on the road. It was one of the scraps of Don's junior high school life that became a signature memory of his friends.

Ruth's predecessor in the Pacific regional leadership of the Women's World Fellowship of Open Bible was Alys Klapstein, wife of Harvey. At that time, the spouse of the regional superintendent was responsible for directing the business of women's ministries. Ruth also gave the ladies strong leadership through the eighteen years she and Milton served in the regional office. She had creative ideas and a flair for the dramatic, which endeared her to the women of the Pacific region. Like her husband, she leaned heavily upon the Spirit of the Lord for ideas and inspiration in her work. In the years prior to building the regional office, there was no space designated for the WWF. With the completion of the new facility, Ruth was thrilled to have her own private space.

The Lord inspired Ruth to conduct a special anointing service for all women of the region. She centered her program on James 5:13-16, which calls for believers to pray and confess their faults to one another and anoint the sick with oil. She gathered a large number of plastic vials, filling them with oil. When retreats were scheduled in each of the six districts, Ruth passed out the vials, sharing from her heart the message of praying, anointing, and confessing to each other. The Holy Spirit blessed each presentation. It was an unforgettable service for these women. Ruth Bryan, former missionary to Trinidad, took this same message to that island, sharing with the women in special services at the San Fernando Open Bible Church.

Ruth saw a need to which she felt the women would respond. There were plans for building a Student Activity Center, including a new chapel, on the EBC campus. This strategic worship center would need to be equipped with a grand piano and other furnishings. It was easy enough to simply send out a letter asking for money, but Ruth thought she would include a little homemade entertainment. She and her son John produced videotapes, which were sent out to all churches of the region. The stage for the video included a grand piano decorated with Liberace-like candelabras. As the camera panned the scene, Ruth entered, formally attired, talking with her invisible audience as she took her seat at the piano.

She told of her musical background, and of the overly strict piano teacher who hit her fingers with a stick if she struck a wrong note. She related how she decided to teach herself, and learned to play, though only in A flat and D flat. On and on she went, testifying of her self-taught abilities and desire to please her audiences. With lavish ceremony she led up to her first work of art, "Onward Christian Soldiers." Displaying great showmanship, she launched into the Christian march, her fingers dancing across the entire the keyboard...a half tone off key. It was awful! But Ruth kept her serious composure, finishing the song with a resounding crash. She then launched into "America the Beautiful." It was the same terrible mess. If the sound had been turned off, you would have thought you were viewing a virtuoso, but alas, the sound was on, and it came in a brutal half-tone short.

Only Ruth could have pulled off such a feat! Accompanying her video was a letter from Almeda Dukes, detailing the fund-raising effort for the new chapel furniture. The women responded with great offerings, which purchased the grand piano and furniture for the beautiful new chapel.

Ruth prepared thoroughly for the talk she was to give the ladies at the Northern California retreat. Before being introduced, the Lord spoke to her, telling her she was not to present her prepared topic. God wanted these women to honor each other. She invited them to come to the microphone and pay homage to another audience member. The speaker asked the person being praised to stand. That lady was then honored by the testimony of a sister in the Lord. Acts of kindness, prayer, sacrificial love, and many other touching words of appreciation were shared. When the dinner bell went off, nobody wished to leave. The cooks kept the food hot, as these women blessed one another with heartwarming stories of hidden acts of kindness suddenly come to light.

When the invitation came from the Anchorage Open Bible Church, Ruth was delighted to go. Milton, who usually traveled with her, was unable to attend. It was special because this was the first women's retreat in Alaska. As usual, Ruth and the women had a great time together that weekend. On the flight home, her plane landed in Juneau to pick up several passengers, including a young man who sat next to her. As the plane ascended, the cabin pressure began causing excruciating pain in this man's ears. The stewardess came to his side, asking if he would like a strong aspirin. While she was locating medication, Ruth offered to pray for him. He was in so much pain it wouldn't have made much sense to refuse. Following Ruth's prayer, God gave him immediate relief and freedom from pain. It was also a great testimony to the stewardess, who returned with an aspirin that was no longer needed. Ruth trusted God and her husband's teaching: "The enabling comes with the doing." Throughout her life, she has practiced stepping out and trusting God for His results through her faithfulness.

Every other year the Pacific Regional Board traveled out of the country for its meeting. In the fall of 1986, the business meeting was held at a hotel in Mexico. Upon their return, Milton called an Oregon district meeting in Klamath Falls. As they arrived for the business of the district, Milton was ill. He tried to stick it out, but by the middle of the session, he was hurting all over. His men could see he was deathly pale.

Turning the meeting over to one of the other men, Milton excused himself, returning to his motel. Skip Ringseth felt Milton was too sick to be left alone, so he followed him to his motel. Entering the room, Skip could see he was not doing at all well, and worse, there was blood on the floor. Before doing anything, Skip called 911.

Arriving at the hospital, Milton was taken to the emergency room where the doctor began his examination and testing. Milton's entire body was poisoned. Skip was told that if Milton had arrived half an hour later, they could not have saved him. He was diagnosed with gram-negative septicemia, caused by an inflamed prostate. Could it have been something picked up in Mexico?

He was hospitalized for over a week in Klamath Falls. While there, one of his young Open Bible Churches' pastors from a small area church came to visit him. He might as well have been one of Job's friends as he dutifully told Milton, "My brother had what you have, and he died!" The young man didn't even offer to pray for him before leaving.

The doctor in Klamath Falls would not release Milton until he was sure a physician in Eugene had officially taken him under his care. Don Bryan made the trip across the mountains, picked up Milton and drove him to the physician's office in Eugene. Following a short exam, the doctor placed him in the hospital. The original diagnosis was confirmed, pointing to prostate inflammation as the source of the gram-negative septicemia. Milton suffered through prostate surgery. When he continued to bleed, a second operation was undertaken. It was an agonizing struggle for recovery, and Milton, at sixty-six years of age, began to recognize his vulnerability. Ruth had never seen him look so tough. It was a number of months before he began feeling reasonably well.

Milton made a mission trip to Mexico where he preached for Paul Canfield in La Quemada. Later, he received an invitation to speak at a Presbyterian mission outreach in a remote town thirty miles northeast of Oaxaca in southern Mexico. Milton and Ruth invited their son John to accompany them on this venture. The church, pastored by Bill and Jean Emry, met in an abandoned Spanish fort in the little village of Ixtlan de Juarez. The people, standing only five feet tall, came from a number of remote areas, bringing their food and woven reed sleeping mats. Spreading the mats over the baked-clay tile floor, the ladies served handmade tortillas with soup in clay bowls. No spoons or forks were used. They dipped their tortillas in the soup, making a meal out of the simple foods they had brought. At night when some left to return home, tightly rolled newspapers served as torches to light the pathway to their primitive huts. Those remaining slept on the old fort floor.

For the first time in his ministry, Milton tried to preach through an interpreter. Pastor Emry translated after each sentence or phrase. It took awhile to get into the rhythm of preaching, but Milton improved each time he spoke during that week. While translating, Pastor Emry often got anointed and blessed right along with Milton, shouting and waving his arms as he interpreted Milton's words to the congregation.

Praying for the sick and needy here proved challenging for Milton. In such an unstructured environment, his congregation was excitedly talking to each other in Spanish while he was attempting to communicate with those needing prayer. The cacophony nearly drove him to distraction. One lady brought her sick little boy in her arms to be prayed for. Milton laid hands on the child, offering prayer for his healing. The same was done for many others wanting prayer, but it was nearly impossible to recognize the results of God's work among the people.

Upon the family's return to Oregon, Bill and Jean wrote to the Stewarts, thanking them for coming. They reported a number had been healed and the entire congregation had been encouraged by the gospel messages he brought. Among the healings reported was that of the child brought in his mother's arms. This youngster, unbeknown to Milton, had had a growth the size of a grapefruit on his abdomen. After prayer, it instantly disappeared. There was great joy among those wonderful believers.

Milton and Ruth made several missionary trips to Jamaica and Trinidad while serving in the regional office. Just like they did in the States, the Stewarts would bless these congregations with cornet and violin specials. The people spoke proper Jamaican English, eliminating most communication problems, and the Christians coming to hear the Gospel were intent on receiving God's Word, not allowing Milton's American accent to distract them. Pastor Henry, superintendent of the churches on the island, did have a word of correction for Milton. Taking him aside following a meeting, he informed him, "Here in Jamaica we raise corn, but we rear children."

While preaching for the missionaries in Spanish Town, Jamaica, Cedric Lu, a Chinese merchant, answered the altar call, giving his heart to the Lord. Mr. Lu owned and operated several businesses in the area. As Open Bible Church missionaries, Art and Elizabeth Henderson nurtured him, and he grew rapidly in his faith, desiring to share the Gospel with others. Within a few years, he sold his stores and began preaching in a rural hill community. The church he planted thrived. When Milton and Ruth revisited Jamaica, they had the privilege of preaching to Cedric Lu's congregation. What a rewarding experience!

There was one special vacation Milton had in mind for his wife. He knew nothing would please Ruth more than to visit the homeland of her father. Etched in her heart were the memories of many stories her father had told of his native Northern Ireland: the landscapes, people, and Irish customs from his boyhood years. Ruth and Milton planned this trip with the excitement of honeymooners. His eighteen years of mileage-plus credits gave them first-class seats and paid for their entire trip. As the plane from London began its descent into Belfast, Ruth patted Milton's leg and beamed, "Well, dear, we are finally in the Holy Land!" By the time the plane's wheels touched down, Ruth was weeping with emotion.

Milton rented a car for their trip into Belfast. Driving on the left side of the road played with his head for time, but when they left the next morning for the small village of Ballinamallard, county Fermanagh, Northern Ireland, Milton felt comfortable. Ruth's father had been raised in this community. The couple stayed with a cousin they had never met, and the week was filled with tours and the royal treatment from these hospitable people. From their cousin's general store, Ruth was given a Belleek porcelain candlestick. Walking the streets her father had known as a boy was inexpressibly delightful. And the incredible stories told about Grandma Phair, expressed only as the Irish can, enthralled them both. Her father's godly mother had raised her children to live for Him. Her apron pockets were always filled with candy, which was showered upon the neighborhood children she dearly loved. Her parting words to her son as he left for America had been, "Never leave the Lord!" Ruth and Milton bonded with these gracious Christian family members with a love that continues to this day. The first leg of this European trip became history, as the Stewarts flew back to London to meet their friends, the Bryans, for the remainder of their planned tour.

Landing in London, they were united with the Bryans only to discover a hitch in their plans. Inadvertently, they had booked themselves on a tour designed for participants 20 to 30 years of age. Their organizer told them they would be happy to allow them to go on this fourteen-country tour, if they felt they could keep up. A majority of the participants were from Australia, with Canadians and Africans completing the group. The Stewarts and Bryans looked forward to some good cross-cultural experiences. They committed to continue. Hitting it off very well with these young couples, they engaged in a lot of good-natured teasing over accents, or lack of them. Ruth assumed the role of "Mother Superior," letting the younger folks know they could receive counsel from her at any time. It was no secret the Stewarts and Bryans were Christians, and Ruth found herself in several counseling roles during their trip.

Communication problems between two language groups sometimes make for unforgettable surprises. When the Stewarts, Bryans, and the Bryans' son, Mark, sat down in a Paris cafe to have something to eat, Ruth Stewart ordered mousse. That was all she wanted. It had been in the back of her mind for days, and now that she was in Paris, France, she was ready to have the best. When the waiter arrived with their orders, a huge bowl of mousse was set before Ruth. She couldn't believe the size of it! Something had gotten mixed up in translation and there was enough dessert to more than feed the entire group of five. They laughed so hard, they nearly cried. When the tour concluded, they all felt it was one of the best trips ever.

Milton thought deeply about his role as Pacific regional superintendent. He and Ruth had led the region for seventeen years, thanking God for the support of the pastors and their spouses. It had been genuine, with few detractors. Finally, in the spring of 1986, Milton let his regional board members know, "When my term of office expires a year from now, I will not run again." The last months flew by with incredible speed for the couple. God's peace reigned in their hearts.

When the regional board gathered the next spring in Eugene for Milton's final session with them, the board hosted a noon dinner at the local Thunderbird Hotel to honor their superintendent and wife. District superintendents brought lovely gifts for both Milton and Ruth, giving tributes of praise and honor to them for their eighteen years of service and love. It was difficult for emcees Norman and Norma LeLaCheur to shorten the testimonial time. National superintendent Ray Smith said he had never in his life seen such a display of honor given to anyone as was expressed toward the Stewarts. Topping off the ceremonies was the presentation of an oil portrait of the Stewarts, painted by Joniele Emery. This beautiful portrait will have its permanent home in Stewart Chapel, the recently dedicated sanctuary for students of Eugene Bible College.

Milton and Ruth Stewart are leaving an inspiring legacy for us all. Through their entire ministry, they have lived wholeheartedly for Jesus Christ. Their love for God, His Word, their family, and the people they served, knew no bounds. Living the normal Christian life for them was walking daily in the presence of the Holy Spirit and being obedient to His Word. As their years of public ministry came to an end, their heartfelt prayer was an echo of Moses in Psalm 90:17:

"May the favor of the Lord our God rest upon us; establish the work of our hands for us—yes, establish the work of our hands."

* * *

Epilogue

*"But the Lord stood at my side and gave me
strength, so that through me the message
might be fully proclaimed..."*
2 Timothy 4:17

After resigning from the Pacific regional office of OBC, Milton and Ruth continued to live in their Eugene home. Milton accepted many invitations to preach in churches all over the country and in his favorite mission field, San Fernando, Trinidad. He continued to serve as assistant superintendent of OBC an additional four years, through 1991, attending board meetings in Des Moines, Iowa.

Two years later, Ruth and Milton went through an unexpected trial, unrelated to their ministry. They faced wrongful accusations, and the matter was concluded only after significant loss of their financial resources. This incident tested their capacity to "Forgive as the Lord forgave you" (Colossians 3:13). They did forgive those who wronged them in this matter. It was a great comfort having family and friends with whom they could share. Nevertheless, they began making alternative plans for retirement.

Ruth knew something was wrong when she got up that November morning in 1994. Returning from the bathroom, she found her husband on the floor. He was dead weight, unable to move himself, and she could not budge him. Ruth called 911, then reached Pam in Monterrey, who caught the next flight to Eugene. Milton had suffered a stroke, affecting the left side of his body. The first few hours were very tense as the doctors worked on Milton. Over 200 calls came into the hospital switchboards. Visitors began pouring in, so much that the doctor ordered them out and posted "No Visitors" signs. Such an influx of people would only obstruct Milton's recovery. One person allowed at Milton's bedside was Don Bryan. There was a special anointing on Don as he came out to meet the family. "Ruth," he said, "the Lord told me to tell you he is going to live and not die."

And live he did. Physical therapy was begun almost immediately following his two-week hospitalization. Manipulating clothespins on coffee cans, playing catch with Ruth, and learning how to walk through the use of a mirror were all part of recovery. For two months they carried a wheelchair around in the trunk of their car. It was never used. He was stubbornly determined to walk again—unaided. Returning to the doctor's office for a two-month checkup, he walked into the clinic on his own. Bill and Karen Clemons prayed for his left arm, believing

God to make it as strong as his right side. Today, Milton opens jars and uses his left hand for strength tasks. Hallelujah!

While lying on his bed recovering, Milton had uninterrupted time to reflect on his life. Such time was rare even in his semi-retirement. As he had approached death's door, he felt unprepared to stand in the very presence of his holy Savior. There had always been a longing in his spirit to be holy, but he labored under the cloak of the natural man. With time to now meditate and review the many Scriptures he knew on holiness, he came to three profound, but simple conclusions:

1. God is not holy because of what He does. He is holy by virtue of His very nature.
2. Doing holy things does not make you holy. It only leads to self-righteousness.
3. Holiness is entirely God's doing. It is a state of being, infused into thehuman spirit by divine grace and the operation of the Holy Spirit.

Illustration: Iron can be magnetized. By coming into contact with electrical current, iron can, in itself, become a magnet. We can only become holy by the touch of the Divine One. You cannot make yourself holy. In the Old Testament, whatever touched the altar was made holy.

From the equity of the sale of their Eugene residence of 26 years, they purchased a manufactured home in Salinas, California. Their daughter Pam lived in nearby Monterey and could look in on them. The weather was also more temperate. For a number of years, Stewarts were managers of their mobile estate, collecting rent and handling residents' problems. Several years later it became too much of a burden, and they relinquished the responsibility. What they call their "projects" are the people they are actively praying for and attempting to bring to Christ. Neighbors who need prayer or counsel know two people who will love, listen to, and pray for them. Ruth's prayer list, numbering over a hundred, is offered daily before the throne of grace. Milton often takes short walks to visit his neighbors. When a line of trust is established in their friendship, he shares his faith in Christ. Over half a dozen people have come to the Lord through Milton and Ruth's witness there.

Milton has had a number of stents placed in his heart arteries to keep the blood flowing evenly, but has been unable to play his trumpet for several years. Ruth, however, still enjoys her violin, in spite of two open-heart surgeries and having a pacemaker implanted in 2003 to stabilize an erratic heartbeat. The Stewarts are forever young in spirit, upbeat in attitude, and continually reaching out to others.

Ever the active reader, Milton and the author recently discussed a book by Gordon Fee that we both are now reading. It is an exegesis of the Holy Spirit through the writings of Paul titled *God's Empowering Presence*. He is also keenly interested in the development of Eugene Bible College and would love to see the school raise the projected $10,000,000 needed for their endowment fund. When it comes to inheritances and lasting values, there are earthly and eternal. One of the phrases that has stuck in his mind and heart lately is this: "You are what you leave behind." The Stewarts know the financial inheritance for their family members will not be large, but they will leave the memories of lives worthy of emulation, and can look forward to an inheritance in heaven, which will far outweigh any earthly treasure.

This past summer, they gathered with their extended family for a reunion in Eugene. It was a memorable time. Over the same weekend, Eugene Bible College dedicated its new Rexius Event Center. The centerpiece of the second level is the wonderfully-equipped Stewart Chapel, dedicated to M.J. and Ruth Stewart.

Their lives are not yet completed on this earth, but they look for a glorious reunion with all His redeemed ones around the throne of God. As their biographer, I am aware that this brief book is an incomplete story of Milton and Ruth's lives. They have profoundly touched so many; only heaven will reveal the scope of their influence. Hallelujah for two lives well lived!

* * *

Tributes

"I thank my God every time I remember you." Philippians 1:3

I invited friends of the Stewarts to share memories for this book. I regret it was not possible to print all the notes available, but these selected recollections give a personal touch to the story of this remarkable couple.

Ministry to Generations

In November of 1952, I attended my first Youth for Christ rally in Lewiston, Idaho. Thrilled with the program, I rarely missed a rally after that. Milton and Ruth Stewart and Van and Alice Jones, who were involved in YFC, really made an impression on me.

Ruth Stewart was so beautiful with her red hair, immaculate clothing, and loving nature. She became my example of the perfect pastor's wife. Later I modeled my own role in the ministry after what I knew of Ruth. She was it!

I remember Brother Stewart's laughter, and can still see him sitting across the table from me when Van and Alice took me with them to eat after Youth for Christ. His eyes always caught my attention because they were so filled with love and laughter. I felt God's love through those eyes. Because of Stewarts, it was easy to know God loves and cares for me.

I was like a sponge, drinking in every word Brother Stewart preached...whether on the platform, walking the aisle, or climbing on the railing! Cherished memories are the times I worked with Brother and Sister Stewart on their radio program. I sang and she played her violin like a professional. So anointed! He was such a man of God and knew what God was saying!

After only a few months of growth under the Stewarts' ministry, I enrolled at Eugene Bible College. In my second year, I met Del Lumbard and we fell in love. Brother Stewart married us on June 2, 1956, at First Christian Church, and Sister Stewart played her violin.

What do the Stewarts mean to Del and me? Del often testified that if M.J. Stewart said, "God told me something," he could believe it as truth more than any thing coming from anyone who claimed to hear the voice of God. The Stewarts became our example in dedication and commitment to Christ. There are no other ministers in OBC that have influenced us so much. They are the epitome of a man and woman of God. Flawless? No. Neither was King David, but he was a man after God's own heart.

Our son, Michael, and his wife, Pam, have found the Stewarts' friendship and hold them in their hearts as we do. They, too, are Open Bible Churches' ministers and pastors. Their two sons think of the Stewarts as spiritual grandparents. From Stewarts' example, we have been able to raise our three sons, Michael, Ric, and Marvin, to know Christ personally and to lay themselves before God in total surrender. All ten of our grandchildren passionately serve Jesus. Two grandsons, Jonathan and Jordan, are Open Bible Churches' ministers.

I am not so certain all of this would have happened had it not been for Milton and Ruth Stewart and Van and Alice Jones. What examples of men and women of God! I could never thank them enough.

Del and Joan Lumbard
Des Moines, Iowa

Ministry of Friendship

We always enjoyed Stewarts' musical talents— Ruth on the violin and Milton on the cornet. Whether it was at one of the churches they pastored, or at a camp meeting, they were always willing to be a blessing musically.

Then, of course, I always loved Brother Stewart's anointed messages. He preached for us when I was regional superintendent, at both our pastors' conferences and our camp meetings.

It was my privilege to have shared rooms with him when we both attended executive board meetings. I remember one time staying at the Sheraton Hotel in Washington, D.C. I asked him if he would save the little boxed soaps that had an "S" for Sheraton stamped on the bar. He was very diligent to give me all his and any others he could pick up. Then on the last day he yelled, "Hey, Smith, it just hit me. My name starts with an 'S' too!"

With Brother Stewart around there was never a dull moment. We had many laughs together, and many times of praise, prayer and rejoicing.

Lawrence and Ellen Smith
Denver, Colorado

Ministry by Example

Milton and Ruth are just the best! Milton loved to preach the Word. His inspiration rarely took him beyond his introduction, with more great points to come in the messages that followed. Ruth demonstrated how to produce musicals and events, skills my wife and I have used down through the years. I literally had a stage set built, like the one she used in "Night of Miracles," to tell the story of Jesus to the Christmas crowds. Anointing rested upon this couple no matter where they were or what they were doing.

The Stewarts were pastors of Lighthouse Temple when I met my wife, Wilda. We had special Wednesday night meetings of prayer, and the power of God was so very evident. Even as young college students, we did not want to miss those services. Following the Wednesday night meeting, we were sure God would move upon all of us as we waited upon Him in the prayer room. The frosting on the cake was the blessing of taking two classes taught by them at Eugene Bible College, "Pentecostal Truths" and "Prayer Life." Life-long tools were given to us from the lessons out of their hearts.

We observed them both being led in their relationship with Jesus in all they did. They shared their personal relationship with our Lord with all of us younger ministers. Their kindness and hospitality were seen and experienced by many. Ruth is a classy lady, current in style and presentation. Milton tells the story of polishing the heels of shoes, making sure all the details were covered. Someone would be looking. Their style and demonstration revealed how we should all strive to serve Jesus in our lives.

We were privileged to serve on the regional board, under Milton's leadership. I continued that service for twenty-five years. M.J. and Ruth had performed our wedding at First Church of the Open Bible in Portland. Twenty-five years later, as we celebrated our 25th anniversary, they traveled to Tacoma, Washington, to be with us. They are special people in our lives.

Doug and Wilda Trentham
Sunnyvale, California

Miracles, Missions, and Ministry

Brother and Sister Stewart were our awesome pastors at Peoples Church in Ventura, California in the early '60s. How special they were! I experienced two miracle healings through their ministry. Following the birth of our second child, I developed problems and was scheduled to have a hysterectomy. On a Sunday morning at the altar, Brother Stewart prayed for me. I was healed and able to cancel the surgery. Later, I struggled with a great spirit of fear. I felt someone was following me. Nightmares and depression were common. I explained my situation to the Stewarts and they prayed with authority over my life. God gave me a great deliverance.

It was because of the Stewarts and Don and Ruth Bryan that my husband and I came into OBC. We have been OBC pastors for nearly thirty years, ten of them as Open Bible Churches' missionaries to Mexico. The Stewarts have been such encouragers all through our ministry. They believed in us when we had no confidence in ourselves. They were mentors to us, especially in our spiritual growth. All through our lives, as Christians and as His ministers, the Stewarts have been so instrumental in loving us and exemplifying to us great Christian grace.

As pastors they have been welcomed in our home and were frequent speakers at our church in Oregon. When Brother Stewart needed a break, he could always come and stay with us. Brother and Sister Stewart are great people of God.

Bill and Fayth McConnell
Missionaries to Mexico

Ministry of Powerful Prayers

Milton Stewart was Pacific Regional Superintendent in 1985 when we planted a church in Arizona. He instantly became a spiritual father for me. Since he has a daughter named Pam, he called me his other Pam.

One day while planting the church in Arizona, my life had become overwhelming. I remember thinking, "Who can I call to pray for me?" Brother Stewart is the one I thought to call. When I got him on the line, I poured out my heart and cried. He encouraged me and prayed for me right then. I felt much better and, later that week, some money came in the mail from the Open Bible Churches' Pacific Regional office, which was such a blessing!

Brother Stewart has been one of the greatest encouragers in my life! At one time I was responsible for organizing a women's conference in California (I lived in Arizona then). The women were called to prayer at a special point in the weekend. My own heart was heavily burdened for a difficult situation at work.

As I was praying, I heard a man's voice and turned around to see Brother Stewart! I went over to him, and without even saying a word, he began praying. There was such a release in my spirit, I went home a different woman! Think about this...I am at a women's conference in California, when living in Arizona; Brother Stewart was in California, when living in Oregon; he was the only man in the room at a women's conference! What a memory for me!

Another memory I have of the Stewarts is from the first women's retreat I attended in California. Ruth was the speaker and may have been carrying a few extra pounds. When she got up front, she opened her outside jacket and lifted it as she twirled around. She said, "Okay...let's get it over with. Take a good look, because I don't want you to be thinking about what I look like or what I am wearing while I am talking! I want you to hear what God has given me to share with you." What a lady!

Pam Lumbard
Des Moines, Iowa

Ministry of Healing

Our board at the Open Bible Church in Medford, Oregon, scheduled a Saturday morning breakfast meeting with our regional superintendent, Milton Stewart. Pastor Virgil Harsh introduced each of us to Milton, but when he mentioned my name, he added I had been having some pretty serious back problems. We had our breakfast and as we were leaving, Milton came up to me. I stuck out my hand to shake his, but instead, he just laid his hands on my shoulders and prayed for the healing of my back.

As I went to my pickup and began driving away, I noticed something wasn't normal. Twisting my torso one way, then another, I was shocked that God had actually healed me. I was free of pain and had complete flexibility again in my back. What a great time of rejoicing my wife and I had!

On Sunday morning, I was anxious to see Brother Stewart again to let him know that God had certainly touched me. As I entered the church, Brother Stewart caught sight of me first and literally ran across the entrance of the church to where Jan and I had come in. He grabbed my hand and said, "Say, Frank, God healed you, didn't He?"

I was shocked. "How did you know?" I asked.

Milton replied, "Well, a short time after you left yesterday morning, God spoke to my heart and said, 'I just healed that man!' And I can see that He did. Praise the Lord, Frank. Isn't God good to us?"

Frank and Jan Meadows
Central Point, Oregon

Partners in Ministry

Milton Stewart and I worked together hand-in-glove during the sixteen years I served as president of Eugene Bible College. We traveled thousands of miles by plane and car, ministering in World Evangelism conferences and visiting churches. I witnessed his ministry in a host of situations, from the Eastern and Mountain Plains Regional Conferences to the Pacific Coast Conferences. Milton was usually the featured speaker at the conferences while I led workshops. I also served for two years as his assistant, shortly after he became regional superintendent.

During the thirteen years my wife, Ruth, and I served as missionaries in Trinidad, West Indies, Milton and Ruth came on two occasions to minister at our conferences and revival meetings. Before they ever arrived, they had blessed our mission field with the gift of a large tent, which became invaluable during our years building the church.

God knit our families together during our ministry in Eugene, and my oldest daughter Brenda is married to his son, John.

Don and Ruth Bryan
Eugene, Oregon

Ministry of Consistency

Milton Stewart was such a dynamic preacher. Darwin and I remember him as our pastor for several years in the old Lighthouse Temple. He impacted our lives tremendously. Ruth and Milton were such a team, always so caring. They had a way of making you feel welcome instantly. We remember he would occasionally do the spiritual emphasis at the Bible college.

Even after our time in YWAM, we often mentioned how his way of ministry is not seen so much now. Too often we feel we need to be so 'correct' as not to offend. Milton Stewart laid it all on the line!

Darwin and Anne Newton
University Place (Tacoma), Washington

Ministry of Support

I first heard about Brother Stewart through his radio ministry in Lewiston, Idaho, when I was 12 years old. My family used to listen to his broadcasts. Before long, an area-wide revival broke out in their ministry at Prayer League Tabernacle. Our families attended many of these meetings and were blessed.

One result of this revival followed several years later when the Stewarts pioneered a new Open Bible Church, beginning its services in the Clarkston, Washington VFW building. My good friend, Walt Olinger, and I attended the first service, and before long our families joined us. I remember taking part in cleaning the building early on Sunday mornings for our service. There had usually been a party or dance there on Saturday night.

Before long, the Idaho State Law Library building was purchased for our new Open Bible Church congregation. The example of Stewarts was such that men, women, children and youth all worked together to remodel this building into a wonderful place of worship.

Brother Stewart's strength was not carpentry. Due to his past experiences in this field he would say repeatedly, "Measure twice; cut once!" This saying has influenced me in many ways. I learned to think through things before acting. Good advice, Brother Stewart.

Attending church with Stewarts as pastors was a great experience. Every Sunday morning there was anointed prayer and preaching. Often there were tongues and interpretation of tongues, prayer for the sick, and people at the altar giving their hearts to the Lord. God was so present and real that you could not doubt Him.

Brother Stewart was always encouraging and supportive! Jan and I felt his backing when we stepped out into missions in Mexico, Liberia, and for over twenty years in the Philippines. It is awesome to know there are those back home in the states who can, and do, feel the nudge of the Holy Spirit to pray for you. We always knew we could count on the Stewarts to be the kind of prayer warriors we needed. Brother Stewart went through many ups and downs with Jan and me as we served the Lord in mission work through OBC. We always knew he supported us!!

We are privileged to have known, loved, and worked for the same Lord as the Stewarts! We pray God's blessing continues to be with them.

Paul and Jan Townsend
Springfield, Oregon

Soul Winner to Soul Winner

As a student in Bible college, Milton was an outstanding leader in activities. He was well liked by his teachers, and his grades showed it. He turned into a dynamic preacher who always got results. He inspired two generations of preachers and will be remembered by all.

Fred Hornshuh Jr.
Eugene, Oregon

(Ruth Stewart remembers Fred once said he loved to be in a prayer time with Milton, if for nothing more than to listen to his friend pray.)

Ministry Ongoing

As a junior in high school, I met Brother and Sister Stewart after friends introduced me to the Lord and encouraged me to come to church with them. I can remember how personable the Stewarts were and how I loved going to the Open Bible Church held in the Veterans of Foreign Wars memorial building in Clarkston. I so enjoyed Ruth's playing of the violin and M.J.'s trumpet music. What anointing they had on their talent! It was there I was first slain in the Spirit. Boy, what a contrasting experience after having been raised in the Lutheran church! The Stewarts helped me grow in the Lord.

After high school, I followed friends who left to attend Eugene Bible College. Upon graduation, I married and we responded to Brother Stewart's invitation to join him and Ruth as their associate pastor and church secretary in Ventura, California. Once again they helped mature me in the Lord. The Stewarts have been such an inspiration to me over the years. I will always be grateful for their love for me. They are truly special people.

Sylvia Currin-Marchand
Cougar, Washington

A "Stinker's" Help in Ministry

My husband and I had the privilege of serving as Brother Stewart's associate pastors for nine months in 1968-1969 at Lighthouse Temple in Eugene, Oregon. What an experience that was and how many gems of wisdom we received through him and his wife during that time.

My husband Skip was in Brother Stewart's office with him on the day of the election of the next Pacific Regional Superintendent of OBC. It appeared, by the tenor of the meeting, that Brother Stewart was going to be elected to that position. My husband selfishly said to him, "I am not voting for you," because he did not want him to leave the pastorate of Lighthouse Temple. Brother Stewart's respect for Skip increased that day because he valued his forthrightness. Later he actually did vote for him, realizing it was inevitable that he was the person God wanted in that office.

As this was transpiring, a group of people in Newberg, Oregon wanted to start a new full-gospel church under the auspices of a recognized organization. Sixty of them had broken away from another full-gospel church in Newberg. They contacted Brother Stewart, the newly elected superintendent, asking him for pastoral recommendations. Since Milton had resigned as head pastor of Lighthouse Temple, it was protocol for his staff also to submit their letters of resignation, making us available.

Brother Stewart asked us if we would go to Newberg to hold services for them. He told my husband, "There are no strings attached concerning you going there to pastor. Just go and hold it open for OBC." However, what the stinker didn't tell us was that he had told the Newberg people he had just the couple in mind for the church!

We were told that they would try out at least four men before choosing their new pastor. That was fine with us, because we weren't going there to pastor anyway. We were holding the church group open for OBC.

After the second Sunday Skip preached in Newberg, he said, "I think they are going to vote on us to become their pastors. We need to be ready." We put a fleece before the Lord, asking Him to give us a unanimous vote if we were to go there. That following Wednesday, we received a call from one of the members saying they had voted on us and were inviting us to be their pastors. My husband said, "I must ask, what was the vote?" The gentleman replied, "It was unanimous!"

It is plain to see that meeting the Stewarts was a divine encounter for us. They have been a real part of our lives. Repeatedly, they remind us of their daily prayers for us. I am always so moved when Brother Stewart takes my husband by the hand and says, "You are like a son to me. You know that, don't you?"

My husband served as Columbia River district superintendent on the regional board for about twenty-five years, beginning with Brother Stewart as his "boss." I had the privilege of serving as district Women's World Fellowship leader, over the same period, with Sister Stewart as my Pacific Division leader.

Personal Note: Brother and Sister Stewart, only heaven can adequately reveal the impact you have had on our lives. May the Lord abundantly return to you the unselfish love and care you have always shown to others. Please be exercising your necks daily while here on earth so your heads won't topple over from the weight of the many crowns you'll receive in heaven.

We love you dearly,

James (Skip) and Dawn Ringseth
Temecula, California

The Real Deal

I first met Milton and Ruth Stewart when they came to speak at First Open Bible Church in Spokane, Washington. I was in grade school and having been raised in church from birth, you know pretty early on who is real and who isn't. Milton and Ruth were the real deal. Whether I saw them in a church setting, at church camp, conferences, or wherever, they were always the same. After meeting them for the first time, they make you feel like you have known them all your life. Milton was someone Jesus shone through; he could preach a fire and brimstone sermon, do it loudly, and not be scary. He always had a smile on his face, was very friendly and loving.

When I went to Eugene Bible College in 1974–1975, I began looking for work. My pastor Norm LeLaCheur called to ask if I would be interested in working for Milton Stewart, who was regional superintendent at the time. I'm glad I said I would. Brother Stewart was a wonderful boss, having a lot of patience with me. I not only learned how the regional business office was run, but, more importantly, I saw how much he loved and cared for every pastor in the division. He was a true pastor's pastor, and took the role of mentoring very seriously. It was such a testimony to see him ministering to those who were on the front lines of ministry every day. And, true to form, when I resigned from my position with him, he gave me a gift and a very nice goodbye card. It was so encouraging to me.

Brother and Sister Stewart are amazing people. Now that Mark and I are in ministry as pastors, we especially appreciate the role they played as encouragers and mentors to us. We have an incredible amount of respect for both of them. They are part of that very rich heritage of godly men and women in OBC, and each testimony is a great source of encouragement.

Mark and Julie Quezada
Baldwin Park Open Bible Church
Baldwin Park, California

Ministry of Mentoring

Although we have been blessed with the friendships of many Open Bible Churches' leaders and peers, no one has made a greater impact, more dramatically influenced, or provided more priceless mentoring/fathering to us, than "Dad" Stewart.

This gift of God came into our lives when my wife Karen and I began Bible college in 1972. Sister Stewart taught the prayer class and Brother Stewart, our Pacific Region Superintendent, was a frequent speaker in chapel.

My Presbyterian upbringing and brief exposure to Pentecostal preaching did not prepare me for my first chapel with Brother Stewart. His informal beginning, apparent musings and meanderings in his "introduction" led me to believe I might be able to get a little well-deserved shut-eye while sitting near the back of the room. That silly notion was soon dispelled.

Nugget after nugget of spiritual truth appeared in what I at first thought were disconnected ramblings. Anyone who thought *that* simply wasn't paying attention. The spiritual pace of teaching, revelation, and prophetic preaching increased with the volume and energy with which he spoke. I had never seen a pastor jump in the air while preaching, and I knew instantly it was not for show or emphasis, but out of unabated passion and anointing.

This was no ordinary man, not at least like any man I had known. In him, mixed in equal portions of passion, zeal and fire, was amazing, poured-from-the-heart-of-God love. I was...we all were...captivated. We thought it a joy to "sit at his feet" whenever he spoke in chapel. Little did we know how our relationship would grow into more than that of a teacher and his disciples.

Before someone accuses me of idol worship, let me say that I know Brother Stewart is just a man. He has faults and weaknesses; he is simply a clay vessel and is but a reflection of the true Light. But he is a remarkable reflection, nonetheless. Following graduation, we went on staff in the Tujunga, California Open Bible Church. To our joy, our pastor invited Brother Stewart to speak several times during our tenure there. In one of those sermons, he imparted the greatest gift of truth any man has ever given me—a revelation of the "cross principle." Jesus Himself might as well have preached it, such was its impact. We received a revelation of the heart of God!

Brother Stewart says his "connection" to us was during a family camp in Southern California in the mid '70s where he spoke in the evening and I in the morning. God knit his heart to ours then, and we have cultivated a rich and intimate relationship to this day.

It was during our first pastorate we began to expand our relationship with the Stewarts. Since I was the pastor, I got to choose speakers, and frequently I had Brother Stewart for special services and retreats. Those times together, as well as his help and ministry to us during and after a major church split, helped crystallize our friendship.

God also used some trying times for Brother Stewart to deepen our relationship. He was receiving a lot of grief from several pastors, some of whom even sent him "hate" mail. We hurt for Milton and Ruth. My wife Karen was praying about it and asked God, "Where is their reward? Is this what they get for their selfless and anointed ministry? Grief? Where is their reward in this life? I know they will receive a reward in heaven, but what about now?"

God altered the state of our relationship with four words, "You be their reward!" And that's what we did. We began to serve them in any and every way we could, whenever we could. We asked nothing in return, because it was a pure joy to serve and minister to them. Their hearts were touched and knit even more to ours, because we weren't doing it to curry favor. Our ministry to them continues to this day, as opportunity allows.

We adopted them in our hearts as parents. Many years ago, after they left the regional office, they adopted us into their family with a formal adoption ceremony. We still treasure the homemade adoption certificate they gave us.

Our lives have been forever changed, edified, and blessed by the lives of Brother and Sister Stewart. He not only taught us the cross principle, he lives it before us. That can be said of few people.

Bill and Karen Clemons
Edmonds, Washington

* * *

Addendum

"Unless the Lord builds the house, its builders labor in vain..." Psalm 127:1

Transformation of Eugene Bible College

What was accomplished at Eugene Bible College over the four years following Don Bryan's appointment as president in 1971, was nothing short of miraculous. This quantum leap forward was bathed in prayer and incredibly hard work. Although Milton was not the hands-on leader of the college, he was the visionary leader of the region and chairman of the regional board, so his support was underlying throughout.

Land and a Dream

During the early years Ed Wood was at the school, he diligently looked for land on which a new campus could be built. The classrooms in downtown Eugene were contained in an inadequate three-story concrete block building next to Lighthouse Temple. Classrooms occupied the two main floors with the chapel downstairs. Some loosely built additions behind the block structure housed a snack bar/student center, music room, and storage rooms. Men and women's dormitories were older homes, reconfigured to house a maximum of students. These were located roughly within a mile east of the main building. The basement of one of the girls' dorms had been remodeled and equipped with kitchen and dining facilities. For their forty years of ministry, the college had seen its piecemeal campus change a number of times. Ed Wood knew that for the school to grow, reaching its potential, they had to develop a campus large enough for all its programs.

Ed sold an apartment building owned by EBC, which had been built as an investment during Harvey Klapstein's leadership. With this money, the regional board purchased a 13.3-acre parcel off Bailey Hill Road, west of Eugene. The property overlooked the city, its beautiful rolling landscape offering a 180° view to the north. The land was dedicated with a groundbreaking ceremony on October 19, 1967. Architectural plans were drawn and Ed began fund raising for the new campus buildings. As diligent and dedicated to the task as he was, there is no explanation as to why the project did not fully succeed. It simply wasn't in God's timing—yet. There was not a shadow of controversy involving Ed or any leaders of this effort. Their hearts and motives were right, but the needed money did not come. After six years as president of Eugene Bible College, Ed resigned in

1971, leaving from his efforts, $105,000 in the bank, an artist's drawing of five campus buildings, and blueprints of the administration building.

The Challenge

Don Bryan had served at the school as executive vice president for two years with Ed, so it was a natural fit for him to assume the duties of president. Not only were there large shoes to fill, but the regional board had made a list of four specific goals they wished to see accomplished. There were no timetables, but—the sooner, the better.

1. Expand the curriculum of EBC, changing it from a three-year diploma-granting Bible school to a four-year degree-conferring Bible college program offering degrees in Pastoral Studies, Christian Education, Missions, and Sacred Music
2. Develop the newly purchased campus acreage
3. Obtain accreditation with the Accrediting Association of Bible Colleges (AABC), recognized by the U.S. Department of Education
4. Be approved by the Oregon Office of Degree Authorization for granting bachelor degrees

Although the board had given no timelines in 1971, Don gave himself two years to have finances in hand and each of the other goals on track for completion.

The Leaders

Few people were qualified to shoulder such a challenge, and fewer could outwork Don Bryan. He learned right away that being a college president was a 24/7 assignment. He began to feel he was fitting the classic definition of this office: "A bag of wind by day, and a ball of fire by night!" Milton helped from his regional office, but Don needed someone qualified to assist in leading the school while he was away fund raising and taking care of off-campus business. Don found his man in Clayton Crymes, who had graduated with a master's degree from Seattle Pacific College.

Milton could not have been more pleased with the selection. He had known Clayton and his wife, Suzanne, since they were young people at the Gold Bar, Washington camp. They too had been fooled by Milton's park ranger costume and speech as described in this book's preface. Clayton became the new Dean of Academic Affairs, competently directing the programs of the college as well as filling Don's shoes in his absence. Two later additions to the faculty were the Burke brothers, Larry and Lonnie, both highly respected by Milton.

Financing Construction

The clouds hovering over the building program of EBC were troublesome when Don became president of the college in 1971. The building plans were stuck in the city's planning commission. Officials were stymied by an Illinois architectural firm's existing proposed plans for a round building. Ed Wood had recently hired a Portland architect to effect a design change, making the buildings sixteen-sided. This new architect also redesigned the original plans to provide more functional and aesthetically pleasing campus structures. Within a year, the new plans were approved. Don could now begin working on the financial package of the campus development.

He began his quest for a building loan by applying at the U.S. National Bank, which the school had used for years. He was turned down. Following this initial rejection, submittals were made to nine different financial institutions from the West Coast to Des Moines, Iowa. Rejection came nine times. Returning to U.S. National, he reapplied, but again was refused. Byron Whisler, a local Open Bible church pastor, suggested Don contact a member of his church for help. Euvon Sanders, who also banked with U.S. National, accompanied Don to the bank, asking the loan officers what EBC needed to do to obtain the loan. The officers replied, "Give us a more detailed presentation including a five-year review of enrollment and finances plus a three-year projection of the same."

Four days later, Don returned to the bank with the recommended report, complete with binder, flip pages and all the essential history and details. The officers told the men they had never seen a finer presentation, asking to keep the report to use as an example for others seeking building loans. In spite of all this effort, the bank, for the third time, turned them down.

Don requested a meeting with the officers, bringing with him, Milton Stewart, regional superintendent, Earl Dukes, board member, and Euvon Sanders. They finally got down to the two essential things over which the bank was stumbling. If EBC would do these, they could have the loan as requested. 1. Present information showing the stability of the regional board structure. This requirement was satisfied on the spot. 2. Have on deposit $125,000. This represented half the construction loan, showing their viability to repay the money. Verifying with the officers that if the deposited money totaled $125,000, the loan would be granted, the men left the meeting.

It seemingly didn't get any easier for Don when the regional board refused to allow him to solicit churches for the additional $20,000 needed. The men immersed themselves in prayer. God was leading, but where were the open doors? The answer came through an incidental call to Don from a realtor asking for a listing on the five dormitories and downtown classroom building EBC would sell when their new campus was completed. When the realtor heard the houses for sale were being used as dormitories, he asked Don if the school was paying taxes on the properties. The positive reply brought a startling fact to light. The University of Oregon pays no taxes on dormitories. The realtor volunteered to call a contact he had at the University who would then call Don and explain the tax laws regarding dormitories. Don was also given the name of the exact person he needed to see at city hall to remove the college from the tax rolls.

Making an appointment with this key city employee, Don brought all the school's tax documents with him and presented his case. After looking everything over, she concluded, "You certainly are eligible for exemption. You will shortly receive an official letter to that fact which will save you over $4,000 per year." Don turned to leave, but was stopped in his tracks by her next words. "The school is eligible for a rebate for the past five years you have paid these taxes." She told Don what kind of information to put together requesting the rebate. Don gave his bookkeeper, Senethea Meyers, the necessary information for the refund request. Then, packing his bags, he headed for the national convention in Des Moines, Iowa.

Upon his return from the Midwest, Senethea greeted him at the school with a twinkle in her eye and an envelope from the City of Eugene. Don found the property tax refund check for $21,000 enclosed! With a "Whoopee!" and a "Praise the Lord!" he dashed to U.S. National with the check. The bank officers were good for their word. It was June 1972, and, with building permits and financing in hand, the construction, under contractor Phil Shelley, could begin.

Don Bryan served as President of Eugene Bible College for sixteen years. When the administration building was completed, upon the recommendation of Milton Stewart and approval of the regional board, it was named Bryan Hall. When Milton resigned in 1987 as Pacific regional superintendent, Don assumed that position, serving for twelve years.

Construction

All that existed on the property was a rough gravel road giving access to the future location of campus buildings. The excavation of the site began with the installation of infrastructures including drainage, water, sewer, electricity and roads. Ed Wood had already built an attractive brick and concrete wall at the campus entrance displaying the school name. Over the next year, it was exciting for the students, faculty, and entire city to watch Phil Shelley and his crew give shape to the campus. During this time, the school was able to expand its property through the purchase of two additional parcels, increasing the campus size to twenty acres. Further money was beginning to come in from churches for the necessary furnishing of the buildings. Finally, in November of 1974, with occupancy permits in hand, moving-in day was announced. Eugene Bible College finally occupied their new campus. Now, back to the academic challenges.

Academic Transformation

Clayton and Suzanne Crymes arrived back on the EBC campus in 1972, following successful ministry at Open Bible Institute in San Fernando, Trinidad. Clayton had taught classes at EBC in the mid sixties, and was re-recruited by President Don Bryan to lead the college through the challenging years of academic change as EBC's new Academic Dean.

Clayton's three challenges were daunting: develop a four-year curriculum for the college, acquire approval of the state to grant degrees, and obtain accreditation from the AABC. Laying out the new four-year program was easy compared to its implementation. Each current student had to be tracked so that the classes needed would be available in the time slots the student had open. When Clayton presented his plan to the faculty at the beginning of the 1973 school year, a new faculty member asked, "Do you want discussion on this, or do you want a 'rubber-stamp motion'?" He accepted a rubber-stamp motion, but promised adjustments would be made in the future, as the curriculum was implemented.

Although the basic plan was approved, the ongoing process of scheduling individual students through this new academic maze was most difficult. Thirty years before President Bush began his education program, Clayton was working to see the motto, "No child left behind," fulfilled. Four years later, those students who had continued their enrollment when the redesign began, were successfully graduated. In the spring of 1976, the school issued its first four-year state-approved degree.

Dr. John Mostert of the AABC had visited the school in 1973 to give Eugene Bible College approval to proceed toward accreditation. This allowed Clayton to work simultaneously on the three projects. No stones were left unturned in the examination of the college. When EBC completed its self-study, three large weakness had surfaced, requiring both short- and long-term action: 1. The college needed instructors holding graduate degrees. 2. The library needed considerable expansion. 3. Several core classes were needed in the curriculum to assure students a complete foundation for a four-year degree.

With these requirements, some current faculty members began contemplating a return to school to obtain graduate degrees. Later, Clayton led by example, earning his PhD in Educational Administration from the University of Oregon. Also, early in the accrediting process, the school began requiring incoming faculty to have a master's degree in their teaching area. The new library on campus tripled the capacity of the former one. Milton and Don challenged the Pacific Open Bible Churches to give books to the school library as a Christmas gift. Over 9,000 volumes were donated. Gonzaga University, Western Evangelical Seminary and the Christian Booksellers Association all made significant book contributions to EBC's library. Curriculum adjustments were made throughout the accreditation process to assure continuity and quality.

After three self-studies and untold hours of research, development, and change, Eugene Bible College was granted full accreditation in 1983. The granting of accreditation by the AABC opened the door for EBC students to qualify for the same federal and state school financing available to students in other public or private colleges. This included loans, Pell grants, and work-study funding. Clayton Crymes continued his distinguished career as EBC's Academic Dean and Vice President for Academic

Affairs for a total of twenty-seven years, retiring from full-time work in 1999.

Postscript

During the intense years of college development, Milton Stewart was a positive influence at every step. EBC had no independent board, but was governed by the Pacific Regional Board of Open Bible Churches, where Milton served as chairman. All significant decisions went through his supervision. Everybody at the school knew Milton was 100% supportive of the ministry of Eugene Bible College. For a number of years, he took the faculty to dinner at the end of the school year. He always stood ready to assist, counsel, and support those who so sacrificially were investing themselves in the lives of their students. He often noted the minimum of conflict between the school and the regional board. They prayed through obstacles, differences and delays. God provided a miraculous new college from their efforts.

To Him be the glory.

Printed in the United States
136953LV00001B/2/P